THE
BANK
WAR

THE DIPLOMATIC HERCULES ATTACKING THE POLITICAL HYDRA.

THE
BANK
WAR

Andrew Jackson,
Nicholas Biddle,
and the Fight for
American Finance

PAUL KAHAN

WESTHOLME
Yardley

Frontis: "Political Quixotism shewing the consequences of sleeping in patent magic spectacles The diplomatic Hercules, attacking the poitical hydra / / from a very big picter in the Jinerals Bed-Room, draw'd off from Nater by Zek Downing, Historical Painter to Uncle Jack & Jineral Jackson." [1833] President Jackson, sword in hand, fighting a hydra with many fierce heads labeled "U.S. Bank," "Deposits," "Bribery," "Pensions,", "[...] of the People," and "Corruption of the [...];" he cries out "Stamp the horrid Monster!!! Crush it!!! Nick Biddle!!! Hell & the Devil!!! Bribery & Corruption!!! Assasination!! Fire!! Murder. Murder!! Where are you Major?" He is being restrained by "Major" Jack Downing, who implores him to "Cum along to Bed agin, Jineral, I tell you Biddle aint here, nor the devil nother as I no on." (*Library of Congress*)

First Westholme Paperback 2022

©2016 Paul Kahan

Westholme Publishing, LLC
904 Edgewood Road
Yardley, Pennsylvania 19067
Visit our Web site at www.westholmepublishing.com

ISBN: 978-1-59416-377-7
Also available as an eBook.

Printed in the United States of America.

Contents

Introduction

This book, like so many works of history, sprang from current events. In the wake of the Great Recession of 2008, voices on both the right and the left criticized the Federal Reserve, often arguing that it exercised too much control over the American economy. Some went so far as to call for the Fed's abolition and for the United States to return to the gold standard. A few semesters later, during a lecture on Jacksonianism in my introduction to American history class, a student commented that history was repeating itself, noting that the rhetoric and concerns about the Bank War were reflected in memes he saw on the Internet. When the student asked where he could find out more about the Bank War so as to better understand contemporary events—the section in the textbook was rather anemic—I was at a loss. Though there are many fine recent biographies of Andrew Jackson and excellent studies of the Jacksonian period, the most recent study of the Bank War is nearly fifty years old. When I mentioned this to the student and commented that it was unfortunate that no one had reinterpreted the Bank War in light of current events, he jokingly said, "Well, you should do it." At the time, I was knee-deep in the manuscript that eventually became my third book, *The Homestead Strike: Labor, Violence, and American Industry* and was not looking for any new projects. Nevertheless, the student's comment stuck with me. The result is the book you are holding, a fresh synthesis of the Bank War that reexamines this critical moment in US history in light of current events.

That the Bank War is a crucial turning point in the political history of the United States is unquestionable. As historian David Kinley noted more than a century ago, the conflict over the Bank of the United States was fought "with a violence of partisan feeling that entered . . . [few other] discussions which determined measures that were to be worked into our political life."[1] Though professional historians are well aware of the Bank War's importance to American political and economic history, few Americans today know that the Bank War and its aftermath led to the first congressional censure of a president, the first Senate rejection of a cabinet nominee, the first use of the filibuster in US history, and at least one fatal duel.[2] More broadly, the Bank War retarded the development of a strong central bank in the United States and was therefore indirectly responsible for the financial instability that plagued America during the nineteenth and early twentieth centuries. Finally, the Bank War was the crucible of the Democratic Party, transforming a loosely organized coalition of widely divergent political interests held together largely by patronage and attachment to Jackson into a disciplined and coherent party. Jackson's veto of the bank's recharter in 1832 crystallized those who opposed the president into the Whig Party, which was predicated on opposition to Jackson's expansion of presidential prerogatives, inaugurating the Second Party System. In other words, the Bank War was a critical moment in American political, economic, and cultural history and therefore deserves a fresh narrative history.

The Bank War's two leading characters, Andrew Jackson and Nicholas Biddle, could not have been more different. Whereas Jackson was the frontier lawyer who pulled himself up from poverty by his bootstraps (and, later, the labor of his slaves), Biddle was born to wealth and privilege, the scion of a prominent Pennsylvania family with strong connections to the Keystone State's political elite. Whereas Jackson was an orphan with little formal education, Biddle attended the College of Philadelphia (later the University of Pennsylvania) and the College of New Jersey (later Princeton University) before traveling to Europe. While Jackson was a noted soldier and dueler who for decades carried at least two bullets embedded in his body (one of them, ironically, fired by a man who would be one of Jackson's strongest allies in the Bank War, Thomas Hart Benton), Biddle was an intellectual who came to future President James Monroe's notice because of his participation in a debate at Cambridge University on the differences between modern and ancient Greek dialects. Yet, for all of their differences, the men shared one important trait that had profound implications for American history. As historian Walter B. Smith sagely noted in 1953, "Both parties [to the Bank War] believed themselves motivated by high moral principles and entirely in the right."[3] Illustrating this point, Jackson himself exclaimed, "The golden calf may be worshipped by others but as for myself I will serve the Lord."[4]

Because of the stark differences between Jackson and Biddle and the righteous tone of the debate about the Bank of the United States, historians have frequently described the Bank War in moral terms, as a clash of "good guys" versus "bad," a construction that reflects Jackson's worldview. For instance, historian Arthur M. Schlesinger Jr.'s 1945 classic, *The Age of Jackson*, depicts the Bank War as a conflict between Jacksonians, fighting for the common man (i.e., the good guys) against the entrenched economic elite (the bad guys). According to Schlesinger, the Bank War was nothing less than "a battle between antagonistic philosophies of government: one declaring . . . that property should control the state; the other denying that property had a superior claim to governmental privileges and benefits."[5] For Schlesinger, a partisan Democrat, the battles of Jackson's era mirrored those of Franklin Roosevelt's time, with the Bank War framed as a distant precursor of the New Deal. On the other end of the spectrum is economic historian Bray Hammond, whose 1957 book, *Banks and Politics in America from the Revolution to the Civil*

War, depicted the Jacksonians as greedy upstarts trying to overthrow the bank in order to enrich themselves. Hammond's depiction of the Bank War mirrors Schlesinger's, except with the roles reversed; in Hammond's telling, the Jacksonians are the bad guys, while Biddle is the story's ill-fated hero valiantly (but ultimately futilely) trying to beat back the democratic barbarians at the gate.

My perspective is different. While I would not call Biddle a hero, I am not convinced that the Bank of the United States was a "monster" that needed to be destroyed. If Biddle was the politically naïve technocrat insensible to the changes reshaping the American political landscape, Jackson was the self-righteous ideologue committed, in the face of all evidence to the contrary, to a simplistic and quite frankly wrong view of the value of and need for a central bank in a rapidly industrializing capitalist economy. Furthermore, Jackson had a Manichaean worldview in which people were either with him or against him, and there could be no compromise with those he deemed to be against him. Jackson's perspective militated against compromise and pragmatism, and as the Bank War demonstrates, there was (and is) a cost to such politics; as Smith noted, "Both parties emerged from the [Bank War] worse off than before. The government found itself minus a well-run central bank. It was now dependent on the state banks, and later was forced to experiment with the defective idea of an independent treasury. The Second Bank found itself with a very bad charter from the Commonwealth of Pennsylvania and a mass of not too liquid assets."[6] However, of the two, Jackson played the more important role: it was he who initially politicized the Bank of the United States, and the showdown over the bank's recharter was a direct result of Jackson's ambiguity regarding the administration's goals and his two-faced willingness to say one thing to one person and another thing to another. These characteristics made conflict inevitable.

As I hope *The Bank War* makes clear, Jackson was frequently a prisoner of his own preconceived notions about how the world should work, and nowhere was this clearer than in the Bank War. Biddle, if politically naïve and elitist, nevertheless was a dedicated public servant who pursued policies he thought best for the Bank of the United States and the country as a whole, though in the end he allied himself with men like John C. Calhoun and Henry Clay, who saw the whole affair less as a high-minded debate about the country's economic future and more as an opportunity to defeat Jackson politically and thus advance their own careers. At numerous points in the conflict, Jackson ignored evidence that contradicted his beliefs, pursuing policies that had a disastrous effect on the American economy. At the same time, the president relied on advisers like Martin Van Buren and Roger B. Taney, whose advice was heavily shaped by their own political and economic interests. In a hyperpartisan era in which both sides claimed the moral high ground and political fights were framed in terms of absolute good and unredeemable evil, compromise was impossible.

For a history of the Bank War to have any educational value, a more balanced account that moves beyond heroes versus villains is required. In my view, the Bank War is more than just the story of a confrontation between Andrew Jackson and Nicholas Biddle over the recharter of the Second Bank of United States; in many ways, it is a debate as old as the Republic about the power and influence of the president. I believe that subsequent events, particularly the boom-and-bust cycle of the American economy in the nineteenth century, vindicate his policies and the existence of the Bank of the United States. In addition, the Bank War highlights the ongoing tension between two conflicting ideals in American political history: nonpartisan technocratic policy making and democratic accountability.

As I mentioned at the start of this introduction, contemporary events fueled my desire to write *The Bank War*. In the shadow of a worldwide economic meltdown and in the presence of seemingly endless partisan gridlock, it is easy and comforting to believe that things were better in the past. *The Bank War* is a reminder that this myth, while comforting, is false and that while Harold Pinter was certainly correct in calling the past a "foreign country," they do not do everything differently there. If readers perceive some level of repetition, particularly with regard to debates about the First and Second Banks of the United States, this is intentional; one of *The*

Bank War's themes is the persistence of Americans' ambivalence about central banking and paper money. Though that debate was more or less settled by the creation of the Federal Reserve System in 1913, the proliferation of pundits like Glen Beck encouraging their listeners to buy gold as a hedge against the coming economic melt-down and the Texas legislature's recent decision to create a state gold depository suggest that controversies described in *The Bank War* remain alive and relevant to contemporary Americans.

1

A Bank
for the
United States

Though few Americans are aware of it, debates over paper money and economic policy are as old as America itself. One of the irritants that caused the American Revolution was Britain's economic policy toward the colonies, and once the states won their independence, the debates over the scope of the federal government's power to charter a central bank proved to be some of the most divisive in the early republic. Indeed, the controversy over a central bank gave birth to the first party system in the United States, and though Congress chartered the first Bank of the United States in 1791, it remained a controversial institution until its demise in 1811. One of this chapter's important themes is that in the case of both the first and the second Bank of the United States, its enemies were eventually forced to support it out of necessity; in both the early 1790s and the mid-1810s, the United States faced economic crises that essentially overrode critics' ideological opposition to a federally chartered central bank. This was something that became a trademark of debates about central banking in the United States up to Jackson's presidency; namely, that when push came to shove, pragmatic need frequently overrode ideological objections, frequently making for strange political bedfellows. Those ideological objections, however, never disappeared, and when the original crises that led to the banks' charters abated, there were sustained efforts to abandon the banks.

Beginning in the sixteenth century, England embraced mercantilist policies designed to increase the empire's wealth by aiding English merchants, who were viewed as the government's partners. These policies, which included trade barriers and subsidies, were expanded in the seventeenth century. The dominant assumption of mercantilism was that trade is a zero-sum game, and the vigorous implementation of mercantilist policies was designed to ensure that specie (i.e., precious metal, most often gold and silver) flowed into, but not out of, Great Britain. Parliament even banned the export of specie to the colonies and barred the colonies from minting coins. As a result, the colonies had little cash, and they relied on substitutes (like tobacco or other crops) as money beginning in the 1610s. At the end of the seventeenth century, nine varieties of foreign coin circulated in South Carolina, and this was far from the exception: colonial money was a hodgepodge of foreign coin, most of which circulated at a premium (i.e., a value higher than its face value).[1]

The colonies, prohibited from coining their own money, by 1690 began experimenting with paper money in order to lubricate growing and increasingly complex economies. In that year, the province of Massachusetts Bay authorized the first issuance of paper money in the western world, and the other British colonies soon followed suit. These bills were fiat money, meaning they had value because the issuer declared it so, not because they could be redeemed for specie. The colonies' frequent conflicts with Native Americans, which necessitated high amounts of military spending, coupled with their governments' unwillingness to raise taxes (and thereby lower the number of bills in circulation) contributed to inflation and enraged British merchants, who were forced to accept depreciating colonial paper money for goods they exported to North America. As a result, by the middle of the eighteenth century, Parliament took steps to curtail the colonies' issuance of paper money, most notably through the Currency Acts of 1751 and 1764. The Currency Act of 1751 applied to the New England colonies and severely limited the circumstances under which they could issue paper currency. The act allowed the existing paper currency to be used for public debts (i.e., taxes) but forbade them being used to pay private debts; the goal was to protect Great Britain's merchants from having to accept the deflated paper. In 1764, Parliament extended its attack on paper money to all of the colonies, prohibiting them from making future paper money issues redeemable for either public or private debts. In other words, the colonies could print whatever they wanted, but they could not make the notes legal tender.

Naturally, these tight money policies hurt the colonies' economies and pushed them toward rebellion. This was one of the reasons they reacted so negatively to the various taxes that Parliament passed in the 1760s and early 1770s; in addition to objecting on principle, the colonists recognized that these direct taxes threatened to further diminish the colonies' supplies of specie. In 1774, the First Continental Congress called the Currency Act of 1764 "subversive of American rights" and demanded its repeal, though Parliament had amended the act the previous year to again allow the colonies to emit paper money. Like so many of Parliament's attempts at compromise, it was a case of too little, too late; within months, the British were involved in a shooting war with their former colonies. Banding together in Congress, the colonies—now independent states—drafted a constitution in 1777. Though it was not ratified until 1781, the Articles of Confederation guided Congress's operation during most of the war.

The document's many weaknesses exacerbated the young nation's economic problems. For instance, though the Articles of Confederation were designed to allow the states to prosecute the war for independence in a coordinated fashion, the revolutionaries' fears of strong centralized government ultimately deprived Congress of the powers it needed to achieve victory. For instance, the articles denied Congress any power not expressly granted in the document, and though it granted to Congress the right to issue fiat money, it had no power of taxation or the ability to compel states to contribute to the country's defense. Lacking the ability to levy taxes, Congress financed the war almost entirely on paper, which included bills of credit (essentially IOUs backed by future tax revenue) that circulated as currency. These "continentals," as they became known, quickly depreciated because, having no ability to levy taxes, Congress had no mechanism for eventually redeeming the notes. By 1779, the continentals had depreciated to between one-fifth and one-seventh of their face value, so the following year Congress decreed that the old bills could be exchanged for specie at a rate of about forty-eight continentals to one ounce of silver. Naturally, this brought many of the old bills back to the government, and Congress in turn issued new bills that just as quickly depreciated, eventually reaching a ratio of more than one hundred continentals per ounce of silver.[2] By 1780, Congress was bankrupt, as was the state of Pennsylvania, and continental currency was so depreciated that it circulated at anywhere between five hundred and one thousand to one. In order to help remedy this situation, in July 1780, Pennsylvania financier and former Continental Congressman Robert Morris established the Bank of Pennsylvania, the country's first national bank. Using his contacts in the business community, Morris managed to raise £300,000, and over the next year, the Bank of Pennsylvania purchased supplies for the revolutionary cause. It was succeeded in 1781 by the Bank of North America, which became the United States' de facto central bank.

Once the American War for Independence ended, the states and the Bank of North America faced massive challenges, including a sizable debt (estimated at $40 million) from the war. The states, too, had taken on a great deal of debt prosecuting the war, but many refused to issue paper money because of concerns about inflation. The states' reluctance to issue paper money points to an important characteristic of eighteenth- and nineteenth-century Americans: their ambivalence to paper money. On the one hand, paper money had fueled the US victory in the War for Independence, which was partially fought because of Britain's restrictions on colonial emissions of paper. On the other hand, once the war was over, many of the states adopted the same tight money policies that had so inflamed colonial anger. For instance, in 1786, Rhode Island's Supreme Court went so far as to rule that forcing merchants to accept paper violated the state's constitution.

Worse, many states raised taxes to pay off their debts, draining money from a system already starved for liquidity. In 1783, Congress authorized the payment of taxes with Bank of North America notes, but in 1785, the state of Pennsylvania revoked the institution's charter. Consequently, deflationary pressure made it hard for common people to pay back money they had borrowed during the war, resulting in discontent that exploded into a rebellion in western Massachusetts in summer 1786. Known as Shays' Rebellion, after its leader, Daniel Shays, it was a response to the Massachusetts government's unwillingness to issue paper money and its aggressive efforts to collect back taxes. Though the rebellion was eventually crushed by a privately funded state militia, it led many observers to conclude that the Articles of Confederation required revision because of the confederation government's inability to fund troops to counter the rebellion.

Meeting in summer 1787, delegates from twelve of the thirteen states wrote a constitution that tried to amend the defects in the Articles of Confederation. Whereas Congress had no power to tax under the Articles of Confederation, Article I, Section 8 of the new Constitution empowered the federal government to levy taxes to pay the country's debts and to fund its military. Furthermore, it granted Congress the right to coin money and, in so doing, denied that right to the states. In addition, whereas the Articles of Confederation said the states maintained all rights not expressly granted to Congress, the Constitution did not; though the Tenth Amendment reserved for the states the powers not delegated to the federal government, the failure to include the word *expressly* meant there was some wiggle room when it came to the limits of federal power. This is reinforced by the so-called necessary and proper clause (Article I, Section 8,

Clause 18), which grants Congress the power "To make all Laws which shall be necessary and proper for carrying into Execution the foregoing Powers, and all other Powers vested by this Constitution in the Government of the United States, or in any Department or Officer thereof." The purposeful ambiguity regarding the limits of congressional power created a space for chartering a national bank but also ensured that it would become a battleground in the war over the scope of federal authority.

When George Washington became the United States' first president in spring 1789, he appointed Alexander Hamilton secretary of the Treasury. Then in his early forties, Hamilton had distinguished himself as a soldier during the War for Independence, as New York's delegate to the Constitutional Convention, and as one of the strongest and most vocal supporters of the new Constitution. Crucially, Hamilton was one of the founders of the Bank of New York (he had written its constitution), so he came to the Treasury Department with some background in commercial banking. In September 1789, within months of his becoming secretary of the Treasury, the House of Representatives asked Hamilton to prepare a report outlining suggestions for improving the nation's credit.

Delivered to Congress on January 9, 1790, Hamilton's forty-thousand-word *Report on the Public Credit* was breathtaking in its audacity, outlining a comprehensive plan for reorganizing the nation's debt and establishing the country's credit. Hamilton's plan called for the new federal government to assume the states' debts and to pay those debts at par. This was controversial for two reasons. First, the states had adopted widely disparate approaches to retiring their wartime debts; some had been quite successful doing so while others had not. Taking on the outstanding state debts seemed to reward the states that had been dilatory in retiring their debts. In addition, most of those debts were in the form of bonds. Over the intervening years, those bonds had frequently traded hands, often at a discount. To pay the current holders of the bonds, many of whom were speculators who had purchased the bonds at a discount, seemed to be rewarding speculators at the expense of the patriots who had bought the bonds in the first place. Hamilton's responses to these criticisms were brutally pragmatic: He argued that it would be impossible to track down the original owners of the bonds, and failing to pay the bonds at face value would injure the United States' credit. Regardless of the morality of the issues involved, Hamilton argued, pragmatism demanded doing whatever possible to restore the nation's credit.

Another controversial element in Hamilton's plan was the creation of a central bank. A central bank has a number of important features that distinguish it from commercial banks, the most impor-

Alexander Hamilton. (*Library of Congress*)

tant of which is the ability to regulate the nation's money supply and credit.[3] Historian Robert V. Remini defined commercial banks as "profit seeking, privately owned institutions which create cash deposits payable in legal tender on demand."[4] The Bank of the United States was self-consciously intended to go beyond merely a large commercial bank to be a true central bank, a point Secretary of the Treasury Alexander J. Dallas made in 1815 when discussing the charter of the Second Bank of the United States. Though written nearly a decade after Hamilton's death, and describing the Second Bank of the United States rather than the first, Dallas's words nonetheless capture the essence of Hamilton's vision. According to Dallas, the Bank of the United States

> ought not to be regarded as a commercial bank. It will not operate upon the funds of the stockholders alone, but much more upon the funds of the nation. Its conduct, good or bad, will not affect corporate credit alone, but much more the credit and resources of the government. In fine, it is not an institution created for the purposes of commerce and profit alone, but much more for the purposes of national policy, as an auxiliary in the exercise of some of the highest powers of government.[5]

Specifically, the Bank of the United States would act as the Treasury Department's fiscal agent, collecting revenues and disbursing payments. In this role, the bank would naturally hold the country's specie reserves and was expected to provide a sound national currency. Given these functions, the bank would be the main force regulating commercial credit and the health of the country's banking system.[6]

Hamilton consciously modeled the Bank of the United States on the Bank of England, which Parliament established in 1694 to finance the Nine Years' War. Hamilton called it a "great engine of state," celebrating what he saw as its four main functions: receiving taxes, disbursing government payments, circulating currency, and discounting bills of exchange (a noninterest-bearing promise of future payment similar to a check).[7] Hamilton asserted that the Bank of North America, while it had provided admirable service during the war, was not up to the task of acting as a central bank because it held a state, rather than a federal, charter, and Pennsylvania had imposed a capital restriction on the bank of $2 million. What was needed, Hamilton argued, was a true central bank that could operate in all regions of the country, and such an institution required a federal charter.

Under Hamilton's plan, the Bank of the United States would be privately owned by shareholders, one of whom would be the United States. The bank would issue twenty-five thousand shares at $400 each, for a total capitalization of $10 million. Under the bank's charter, the president of the United States could purchase up to five thousand shares (at a cost of $2 million) on behalf of the United States, while the institution itself was to be governed by a board of twenty-five directors elected by the stockholders, whose votes were commensurate with the number of shares they held. Given that the United States would be one of the bank's largest shareholders, this guaranteed the president substantial control over the composition of its board and therefore its policies. Lest anyone be concerned that Hamilton's plan was simply a scheme to transfer the nation's wealth to the rich and powerful, the secretary of the Treasury assured Congress, "Such a bank is not a mere matter of private property, but a political machine of the greatest importance to the State."[8] In fact, the Bank of the United States was specifically prohibited from trading in anything beyond bills of exchange, bullion, or tangible goods pledged as collateral for loans; in short, it was not a commercial bank.[9] One quarter of the stock's purchase price had to be paid in specie against which the bank would issue notes. Hamilton ensured these notes would circulate as money (and at their face value) by proposing that the bank, which would collect revenues due to the United States, would accept the notes as payment.

What made the plan attractive, at least from Hamilton's perspective, was that it sidestepped what he saw as the downside of representative government, namely, that politicians would be unwilling to make necessary but politically difficult decisions in times of crisis or that they would be tempted to manipulate the money supply for short-term political gain. By contrast, a largely independent Bank of the United States could adjust the country's money supply and regulate credit as circumstances, rather than politics, dictated. Hamilton himself noted, "The stamping of paper is an operation so much easier than the laying of taxes that a Government, in practice of paper emissions, would rarely fail, in any such emergency, to indulge itself too far in the employment of that resource, to avoid, as much as possible, one less auspicious to present popularity."[10] Essentially, Hamilton saw the bank as a hedge against the unpredictability of democracy, and that dynamic—the conflict between technocratic policymaking and democratic accountability—is the basic story of the Bank War.

In addition, a central bank like Hamilton imagined was incompatible with metallism, or the belief that money derives its value from the material of which it is made. Metallists, or advocates of so-called hard money (precious metals minted into coins), opposed any substitute forms of currency (like paper). Hamilton recognized the antimetallist orientation of a central bank and celebrated it, arguing that the Bank of the United States would succeed in "vitalizing as well as economizing the dead stock of gold and silver" in the United States by issuing paper currency. Because paper money was easier and cheaper to manufacture and transport than coins minted of precious metal, the Bank of the United States would reduce government expense and facilitate trade.[11] While this was a positive good as far as Hamilton was concerned, the bank's antimetallist orientation infuriated the many Americans opposed to paper money. These advocates of hard money argued that only gold or silver should be used as cash in the United States, and the popularity of their argument demonstrates Americans' ambivalence about paper currency.

For these reasons, Hamilton's proposal for the Bank of the United States, like his plan to assume the states' debts, was extremely controversial. In 1790, the United States had only three banks—the Bank of North America, the Bank of Massachusetts, and the Bank of New York—so the average American had little experience with these institutions, and his wartime experience with paper money (the heavily depreciated continentals) was negative. Furthermore, some of Hamilton's critics saw it as an attempt by the country's business elite, which was largely centered in the Northeast, to exploit the agrarian South, reflecting the incipient sectionalism that would lead to civil war in less than a century. Still others argued that the bank was unconstitutional because the federal government lacked the power to charter corporations or banks. This argument reflected one of the central debates in American history, that between strict (or literal) and broad interpreters of the Constitution. According to Congressman James Madison, who became one of the most vocal critics of Hamilton's plan, any power not expressly granted to the federal government by the Constitution was reserved to the states. Madison pointed out that nowhere in the Constitution was Congress granted the right to charter a bank, so it lacked the authority to do so. Hamilton argued that the federal government's right to charter the bank was implicit in the "necessary and proper clause" and was essential in order to execute the powers delegated to the federal government, including the right to collect taxes and duties and to borrow money on the credit of the United States,

The fight over Hamilton's economic plan was the most important ingredient in the emergence of political parties in the United States. Though the debate over the ratification of the Constitution led to the emergence of two factions—those who supported the Constitution's ratification were known as Federalists, while those opposed to ratification came to be called Anti-Federalists—these were not political parties per se. In fact, neither supporters nor opponents of the Constitution would have identified themselves as members of a party in 1787 or 1788; it was not until the 1790s when political factions that coalesced around Hamilton and Thomas Jefferson began crystallizing into parties. However, by the mid-1790s, Hamilton's supporters were being identified in the press as "Federalists," in opposition to Jefferson's supporters, who were known variously as "republicans," "democrats," "democratic-republicans," and "Jeffersonians." The Federalists advocated progrowth economic policies that included tariffs and a national bank, all of which were rooted in a vision of America as a modern economic power. The Jeffersonians, by contrast, argued that the federal government was barred from any action not specifically enumerated in the Constitution; they therefore opposed Hamilton's financial policies as unconstitutional. Jefferson's vision was rooted in a belief that America should remain primarily agrarian because farmers were self-sufficient and independent. Writing in 1798, Jefferson expressed the differences between the Federalists and his supporters this way:

> Two political Sects have arisen within the U. S. the one believing that the executive is the branch of our government which the most needs support; the other that like the analogous branch in the English Government, it is already too strong for the republican parts of the Constitution; and therefore in equivocal cases they incline to the legislative powers: the former of these are called federalists, sometimes aristocrats or monocrats, and sometimes tories, after the corresponding sect in the English Government of exactly the same definition: the latter are stiled republicans, whigs, jacobins, anarchists, disorganizers, etc. these terms are in familiar use with most persons[12]

It is therefore somewhat ironic that Jefferson brokered the final passage of Hamilton's financial plan in Congress. Jefferson, then serving as George Washington's secretary of state, invited Madison and Hamilton to a dinner in order to give the two men an opportunity to work out a compromise. Though historians have no definitive record of the discussion, it appears that Hamilton and Madison struck a bargain: in exchange for Hamilton's support of a proposal to move the national capital to the South, Madison would not try to scuttle the bank. Ultimately the Senate approved the bank bill in January 1791, and the House passed it by a vote of thirty-nine to twenty a few weeks later, largely along sectional lines (a foretaste of the role that sectional politics would play in shaping the bank's history). Though Washington considered the bill for two weeks and then asked for his cabinet members' opinions on the legality of the bank, he ultimately signed the bill into law, which granted the Bank of the United States a federal charter to operate for twenty years. It opened its doors for business on December 12, 1791.

Originally headquartered in Carpenters' Hall, in 1797 the bank moved to its own specially constructed building on Third Street between Chestnut Street and Walnut Street. When it opened, the bank was capitalized at $10 million divided into twenty-five thousand shares that sold for $400 each. Subscribers had two years to pay for their shares and were required to pay 25 percent of the purchase price in specie, which served as the bank's reserves against which it could issue notes. By 1805, the bank had five branches spread across the Eastern Seaboard, and, once established, it became an efficient and indispensible adjunct of the Treasury Department, paying government salaries, receiving and disbursing government payments, and lending the federal government money. Though the Bank of the United States was a profit-making enterprise, it paid modest dividends compared to the nation's other three banks. This was no accident: though the Bank of the United States was a profit-making enterprise, its true purpose was to serve the country's interests by providing a national currency and encouraging stable economic growth. Consequently, the Bank of the United States was a more conservative institution than the state banks, whose sole purpose was the highest possible return on investment for their shareholders.

The First Bank of the United States. (*Library of Congress*)

It is important to note that the Bank of the United States was created and operated for its first decade in a very favorable political context. From 1789 to 1801, the Federalists controlled the presidency and the Senate, so the bank's Jeffersonian critics could do little more than carp that the institution was unconstitutional. This changed when Jefferson won the presidential election of 1800 and his allies took control of both houses of Congress in 1803. Historians frequently call the election of 1800 a revolution because Jefferson's ascension to the presidency signaled the beginning of the end of the Federalist Party. Never again would the country elect a Federalist president, and it slid toward one-party rule, at least on the national level. And the Jeffersonians' domination of the federal government posed a serious threat to the bank's interests.

Though Jefferson struck a conciliatory tone in his inaugural address, famously saying, "We are all Republicans, we are all Federalists," as president he acted decisively to undo what he saw as the "monarchical" policies pursued by Presidents Washington and

John Adams. Though Jefferson had brokered the 1790 compromise between Hamilton and Madison that paved the way for the creation of the Bank of the United States, he now worked to undermine the bank in ways similar to those Jackson used a generation later. In 1804, Jefferson sold all of the federal government's stock in the bank at a profit and began depositing federal government funds in state banks, justifying his actions in part by the fact that foreigners owned most of the Bank of the United States stock (rhetoric that Jackson would later use in his attack on the bank).[13]

Despite Jefferson's antagonism toward the bank, the US economy prospered during his first term. From 1803 to 1807, commerce in the United States doubled. However, all of this came to an abrupt end when Congress passed and Jefferson signed the Embargo Act of 1807. The law, which Jefferson had sponsored, aimed to keep the United States neutral in the Napoleonic Wars. Initially, the United States had tried to trade with both sides—the British and the French—but because neither side wanted the other to benefit from American products, both combatants violated American neutrality. The Embargo Act tried to protect American neutrality by forbidding US merchants to export anything from the United States. It was a financial disaster, throwing the United States into a recession and cutting federal government revenue, which was largely derived from tariffs. The year after the Embargo Act became law, American exports shrank by 80 percent and imports declined by 50 percent.[14] The law was such an unquestionable fiasco that Jefferson, humiliatingly, signed a bill repealing the act shortly before he left office in 1809.

However, the repeal of the Embargo Act was in no way the last financial misstep committed by the Republicans during their dominance of the executive branch. Jefferson's successor, James Madison, scored his own impressive series of financial blunders, the most consequential of which was the failure to recharter the Bank of the United States. Congress initially chartered it in 1791 for a period of twenty years, meaning that for the bank to continue, the House would have to pass, and Madison would have to sign, a new charter before the current one expired in 1811. Given Madison's opposition to the bank when it was first chartered and the fact that his party controlled both houses of Congress by overwhelming majorities (28 seats to 6 in the Senate and 106 to 36 in the House), the bank's prospects for recharter seemed dim. So its stockholders tried to mobilize public opinion to pressure the administration into rechartering the bank.

In 1808, a full three years before the bank's charter expired, its stockholders sent Congress a memorial that rehearsed the services the bank provided to the federal government and the country. This memorial asked Congress to recharter the bank despite the fact that Secretary of the Treasury Albert Gallatin has specifically asked the bank's president, Thomas Willing, not to raise the issue of recharter until after the presidential election lest it become politicized. In any event, the memorial languished in Congress until February 1810, when the House Committee on Banking reported favorably on recharter. Although it was debated, the House did not hold a vote on rechartering the bank.

Concerned about the lack of congressional action, in December 1810, the stockholders sent another petition to Congress, which was debated the following month. On January 24, however, the House decided by a single vote to indefinitely postpone consideration of renewing the bank's charter. Two weeks later, a bill rechartering the bank was introduced in the Senate. Over the next two weeks, senators periodically debated the bill, and the argument hinged on two points: the bank's constitutionality and the expediency of having a national bank. The bank's opponents argued that the state banks were more than capable of performing all of the services offered by the Bank of the United States and that the Constitution did not grant Congress the authority to create such an institution. The bank's supporters argued that the Constitution did not specifically forbid such an institution, that the Constitutional Convention's president, George Washington, had signed the bill originally chartering the bank, and that the Bank of the United States was a safer repository for federal government funds than the state banks. In all respects, the debate over recharter mirrored almost exactly the arguments in Congress for and against the Bank of the United States in the early

1830s, though by then some of the first bank's staunchest opponents would become the second bank's most vocal supporters. Ultimately, the Senate voted on the bill on February 20, and the outcome was a tie. Vice President George Clinton voted against recharter. Consequently, the Bank of the United States closed for business on March 3, 1811. Its branches were sold off, with many becoming state banks. The bank's largest stockholder, Philadelphia financier Stephen Girard, acquired its headquarters in Philadelphia and obtained a state charter. Within a year, he was operating the Bank of Stephen Girard from the former Bank of the United States' headquarters.

The Bank of the United States' dissolution in 1811 came at the worst possible time for the country. Political tension between the United States and Great Britain over American trading rights with France, British support of Native Americans in their conflicts with American settlers, and British impressments of American sailors led to increased tension between the two countries. In 1812, following a request from President Madison, Congress declared war with Great Britain, though this declaration was incredibly controversial. On the one hand, a group of congressmen known as war hawks had actively demanded that the Madison administration go to war against Great Britain. Most of the war hawks represented Southern and Western states, and their ranks included Kentuckian Henry Clay, South Carolinians John C. Calhoun and Langdon Cheves, and Tennessean Felix Grundy. Opponents of the war came mostly from the mid-Atlantic and New England states, regions whose economies were based on trade with Great Britain.

During the war, Madison's monetary policies caused widespread inflation, while Britain's blockade of US ports significantly diminished American trade, starving the Treasury of revenue even as war expenditures soared. Without the Bank of the United States, the federal government lacked an institution for mobilizing the country's economic resources against Great Britain. The war was an almost unmitigated military disaster for the United States, and the Madison administration's feckless economic policies made it worse. The government had trouble selling bonds to finance the war, eventually selling only $45 million of the total $61 million authorized. Worse, many of these bonds were sold at below par (i.e., at a discount, which ranged from 12 to 20 percent). This strained the country's finances not only because the federal government was on the hook for interest payments, but when the bonds matured it would have to pay the full face value of the bonds even though they had sold at a discount. A later report concluded that the federal government received only $34 million in specie for loans whose face value totaled $80 million.[15]

In addition, Congress authorized the emission of $5 million of Treasury notes that could be redeemed within a year. As interest-bearing debt instruments, these were more akin to bonds than currency, but they circulated as money, largely because they could be redeemed as payment of duties and federal taxes. Over the next two years, Congress authorized additional emissions of Treasury notes, though when banks along the Eastern Seaboard suspended specie payments in the aftermath of the British burning Washington, these notes quickly depreciated. By summer 1814, the federal government was able to sell only $11.75 million of a $25 million bond issue, most at discounted prices, and by that November, the secretary of the Treasury publicly conceded what many had suspected: the government would not be able to pay the interest on the Treasury notes circulating in New England because it lacked the specie to do so.[16] In sum, Madison's failure to recharter the Bank of the United States and his subsequent decision to go to war wreaked havoc with the country's finances.

The war coincided with two related developments that decisively reshaped America's economy and pointed to the need for a new central bank. The first was the Market Revolution, which was a process by which the United States moved from an agrarian, import-dependent economy to an industrial exporter of finished goods. The Market Revolution's roots were laid during the Industrial Revolution (ca. 1760 to ca. 1840), which increased the mechanization of production and therefore made finished goods cheaper and more plentiful. The federal government's need for weapons and uniforms during the War of 1812 encouraged American domestic industry, which in turn spurred the transition from an agrarian to an industrial economy.

The second development that coincided with the War of 1812 was the massive expansion of the banking sector. Whereas in the 1790s and the first decade of the nineteenth century there were few state banks, the economic expansion caused by the Market Revolution fueled a dramatic increase in the number of state banks. Meanwhile, without a central bank in place to regulate the issuance of notes, state banks flooded the market with paper currency, causing prices to double. Albert Gallatin, the longest-serving secretary of the Treasury in US history, later claimed that the total number of notes in circulation more than doubled, mushrooming from $28 million to $68 million from 1811 to 1816.[17] These notes varied in value from place to place and over time, contributing to runaway inflation. Consequently, people hoarded specie, which virtually disappeared from circulation, leaving only bank notes in circulation. By law, the Treasury secretary was barred from accepting depreciated bank notes, which essentially meant that the government no longer had access to its deposits in state banks. Consequently, the federal government was forced to accept at face value these notes, whose discounts varied wildly. Moreover, the Treasury Department used the state banks to house federal deposits and accept payments, but this was hardly an ideal solution. As historian David Kinley noted, the state banks "proved so unsafe and so false to their trust" that it was soon clear to most observers that another solution had to be found.[18] According to one survey of the period, as late as the 1820s, "A bank could still be chartered and currency notes issued with no other obligation than the printing bill."[19]

The War of 1812, combined with the Market Revolution and the explosive growth in state banking, convinced many foes of the Bank of the United States that the country needed a central bank, though the controversy over the war had an impact on the debate about creating it. On April 2, 1814, Tennessee Representative (and war hawk) Felix Grundy offered a resolution to create a House committee to explore the expediency of chartering a new national bank. Grundy's motion passed the House seventy-six to sixty-nine, and President Madison even (reluctantly) supported the committee's work. When, however, rumors circulated in Washington a week later that the British wanted peace, Madison immediately withdrew his support for the committee's work, and Grundy himself moved that it be disbanded, which the House did. But the rumors proved unfounded; the war dragged on for several months, further damaging the country's economy and credit.

Fortunately, the impetus for a national bank was not dead. Four of the country's most prominent bankers—John Jacob Astor, Stephen Girard, David Parish, and Jacob Barker—strongly advocated the chartering of a new Bank of the United States. In general, these men were motivated by self-interest. The economic upheavals of the Market Revolution and the instability caused by the unchecked proliferation of state banks threatened these bankers' business interests, and they saw the Bank of the United States as an instrument for regulating the country's economic growth. Enthusiasm for a new bank was not limited to the business sector, however; prominent politicians (most of them connected to Pennsylvania) called for the chartering of a new bank in order to help finance the government's war against Great Britain.[20] For instance, in October 1814, Alexander J. Dallas became secretary of the Treasury. Dallas was a Philadelphia lawyer and newspaperman who had served as secretary of the Commonwealth of Pennsylvania from 1791 to 1801 and then as US attorney for the Eastern District of Pennsylvania. Working with the president and members of Madison's cabinet, Dallas developed a plan for a national bank, though he was disappointed when several congressmen who had been friendly to the Bank of the United States opposed his plan largely for political reasons, which was to become an enduring feature of debates over the bank.

One of the bank's most influential and important supporters was South Carolina Senator John C. Calhoun. At this point in his career, Calhoun was a well-known nationalist who was connected to an influential faction of Pennsylvania's Republicans known as the Family Party, a group headed by future Secretary of the Treasury

Samuel Ingham. Calhoun offered his own plan, though it was ultimately disregarded by the congressional banking committee
charged with developing a charter for the bank. In retaliation, he—
along with the bank's future president, Speaker of the House
Langdon Cheves—opposed Dallas's bill. In January 1815, the
Senate voted against Dallas's plan, and when Congress sent
Madison a compromise plan the following week, Dallas said, "I
asked for bread and . . . [Congress] gave me a stone. I asked for a
Bank to serve the Government during the War; and they gave me a
commercial bank to go into operation after the war."[21]

Unhappy with the bill's provisions, Dallas successfully pushed
Madison to veto it. News of the Treaty of Ghent, which ended the
War of 1812, stalled further progress on a bank bill, though Dallas
still believed that peace in no way obviated the need for a central
bank. In December, he and Madison endorsed the need for a central
bank, and thereafter Dallas and Calhoun worked together to craft a
plan that would satisfy each man. In January 1816, Calhoun, now
chairman of special committee exploring the feasibility of a national
currency, reported a bill to create a national bank. Debate on the bill
began on February 28 and continued for more than two weeks. On
March 14, the House passed the bill by a vote of eighty to seventy-
one, while the Senate approved it on April 3, twenty-two to twelve.
Under the terms of its charter, the new bank would operate very
much like the old one. The new Bank of the United States would be
capitalized at $35 million (compared to its predecessor's $10 million), though its shares would sell for only $100 each (compared to
$400 for the first bank). The federal government would again own
one-fifth of the bank's stock, but the bank would have to pay the federal government $1.5 million in three installments. Just as its prede-
cessor, the new bank would have twenty-five directors, five of whom
would be appointed by the president and subject to senatorial confirmation.[22]

During its first year, the bank established nineteen branches (in
addition to its headquarters in Philadelphia) that were not limited to
the Eastern Seaboard. In addition to Baltimore, Washington,
Boston, and New York, branches opened in Lexington and

Louisville, Kentucky, and Cincinnati and Chillicothe, Ohio. By 1830, the bank had twenty-five branches operating. On May 10, 1816, Madison signed the bill chartering the Second Bank of the United States. Many years later, during the fight with Jackson over the bank's recharter, Calhoun claimed "the bank owes as much to me as to any other individual in the country; and I might even add to that, had it not been for my efforts, it would not have been chartered."[23]

That being said, politics, rather than good policy, often dictated legislators' votes. Since the Second Bank was largely viewed as an administration initiative, many of the president's congressional opponents opposed it for no other reason than that Madison supported it. For instance, one influential bank critic was New Hampshire Congressman Daniel Webster, then leading the Federalist minority in Congress. Webster's opposition to the Bank of the United States was political; an opponent of the War of 1812, he opposed the bank because he did not want to give the Madison administration the tools to prosecute the war. To that end, he asserted in January 1815 that "to look to a Bank as a source capable not only of affording a circulation medium to the country but also of supplying the ways and means of carrying on the war—especially at a time when the country is without commerce—is to expect too much than ever will be obtained."[24]

In fact, just as with the War of 1812, geography played an important role in determining how individual legislators voted on the bill: Southerners and Westerners generally voted for the bank, while Northerners voted against it. Madison was partially responsible for this opposition because the president had self-consciously sought to make the bank a Republican institution. His five appointments to its governing board were Republicans distinguished more for their attachment to the party than for any banking expertise. By contrast, the stockholders—almost all of whom were bankers more concerned about financial stability than partisan attachment—appointed an equal mix of Federalists and Republicans; naturally, when joined with Madison's appointees, Republicans dominated the board, and they chose William Jones as the bank's first president.

Jones was a Pennsylvanian statesman who had fought in the American War for Independence. After hostilities ended, he became a successful merchant in South Carolina before entering politics. Elected to the US House as a Republican in 1800, Jones declined Jefferson's offer to become secretary of the Navy in 1801, choosing to remain in Congress until 1803. In 1813, Madison appointed Jones secretary of the Navy, and his policies were an important factor in several key US naval victories during the War of 1812. Amazingly, while serving as secretary of the Navy, Jones was also the administration's de facto secretary of the Treasury because the actual secretary, George W. Campbell, was in bad health. Jones left the cabinet in December 1814, but he returned to public service in 1816 when Madison appointed him president of the Bank of the United States.

Jones's main qualification appears to have been his friendship with Dallas and his acceptability to most of the country's bankers, though Nicholas Biddle's biographer, Thomas Payne Govan, described Jones as "an unsuccessful businessman and inefficient department head . . . who was chosen for political reasons."[25] Prominent Philadelphia banker Stephen Girard (who had purchased the first Bank of the United States when its federal charter expired in 1811) claimed that "corrupt" means had been employed to secure Jones's selection, and throughout Jones's presidency, Girard actively opposed the bank president's agenda.[26] Biddle, who sat on the bank's board of directors, was also unhappy with Jones's ascension to the institution's presidency. Historian Leon Schur has noted that, "Even at its best, Jones's management of the Bank was pedestrian."[27]

Part of the reason for the dissatisfaction with Jones's presidency was rooted in his assumptions about the bank's role in the American economy. From Jones's perspective, the bank's most important obligation was to its stockholders, and he insisted that it should "set a good example" for the state banks by resuming specie payments.[28] One of Jones's first acts as president was to pressure the state banks to resume specie payments, a goal he achieved in late February 1817, though on terms that were unfavorable to the Bank of the

United States. Under the agreement Jones reached with the state banks, the Bank of the United States would immediately become responsible for the state banks' public deposits, but the state banks would not actually be required to transfer the funds to the Bank of the United States until July 1. In other words, the Bank of the United States was lending the state banks millions of dollars interest free for more than four months. In addition, the Bank of the United States agreed not to redeem state bank notes until it had accumulated $6 million worth of notes, and any discounts (i.e., the difference between the notes' face value and the actual amount the bank paid out in specie) would go to the state banks rather than the Bank of the United States. In other words, the state banks could essentially issue bank notes against the Bank of the United States' specie reserves, at least temporarily, and pocket any profit (in the form of discounts) that might accrue.[29]

This was hardly an auspicious beginning to the bank's operation, but it illustrates the intense political and economic pressure the bank faced from the state banks and the Treasury Department. During the 1810s and 1820s, the Treasury Department actively pressured the bank not only to coerce the state banks to resume specie payments but also to open branches in Ohio and Michigan in order to facilitate public land sales. More concerning was the Treasury's pressure to appoint branch directors for political reasons rather than management prowess. Bank President Jones came under enormous pressure to appoint branch directors with "political feelings congenial with those of the [Madison administration]." In an 1817 letter to Jones, Secretary of the Treasury William H. Crawford noted that it was his understanding "that the politics of the bank shall be that of the administration, and that its political character shall change with the government. A regulation of this kind in an institution simply monied, would certainly be wise, with a view to its duration, and prospects."[30]

Pressure to appoint candidates based on their political affiliations was hardly the only challenge facing the Bank of the United States in its first decade. In 1817, the bank opened a branch in Baltimore, and the following year the Maryland legislature passed "an act to impose a tax on all banks, or branches thereof, in the State of Maryland, not chartered by the legislature" that limited the Bank of the United States to issuing notes in denominations of five, ten, twenty, fifty, one hundred, five hundred, and one thousand dollars and imposing a tax on each note issued. In addition, the legislature imposed a fine of $500 for each note issued on which the tax was not paid, half of which was to be paid to anyone who uncovered a violation of the law. The Baltimore branch's head, James W. McCulloch, refused to pay either the tax or the penalty and was sued in state court by John James, a state government official who was trying to claim his half of the fine.

Maryland's Court of Appeals ruled in favor of James, finding that the Bank of the United States was unconstitutional because the Constitution did not specifically empower Congress to incorporate such an institution. As a result, McCulloch appealed the case to the US Supreme Court. In a landmark decision written by Chief Justice John Marshall, the court concluded in *McCulloch v. Maryland* that Congress did have the power to incorporate a national bank, for a few reasons. First, Marshall pointed to the fact that the first Congress had created such an institution. Consequently, he dismissed the argument that only the states had the power to charter banks. He concluded that the Constitution did not explicitly forbid such an institution and that, under the "necessary and proper clause," Congress was empowered to charter an institution designed to help it exercise its powers of taxation. Ultimately, the *McCulloch* decision protected the bank from state taxation and closed debate on its legality for the moment. But as subsequent events would demonstrate, it was not the last word on the issue.

Another challenge facing the bank was the Panic of 1819, the first major peacetime economic crash in American history. The two main causes of the Panic of 1819 were unfavorable balances of trade with European countries and inflationary credit policies that spurred a speculative bubble. The War of 1812, by cutting off US trade with Europe, spurred American industrial growth. Whereas before the war, the United States tended to import manufactured goods, it suddenly became economical (and patriotic) to "buy American."

However, when hostilities ended, European goods came flooding back into the United States, and by 1816, the total value of imported goods was nearly thirty times the value imported in 1811. The United States ran trade deficits in 1815 and 1816, and the country's industrial interests lobbied Congress to institute a protective tariff in 1816. At the same time, the Napoleonic Wars (1803–1815) had devastated Europe's agricultural sector, so Europeans turned to the United States to supply their needs, pushing up the price of cash crops and increasing the demand for arable land. This, coupled with the availability of land seized from Native Americans as a result of the Creek War (1813–1814) set off a speculative boom that created a bubble, even as prices for manufactured goods declined. The land bubble was facilitated by the explosive growth in state banks and the overissuance of notes. In just four years, from 1811 to 1815, the number of state banks more than doubled. During the War of 1812, these banks had loaned the federal government money, and the government had consequently allowed the banks to suspend specie payments. Essentially, the state banks could now issue notes without any regard to the actual amount of specie they held, a practice that contributed to inflation. Many of these banks loaned money (in the form of bank notes) for land purchases, which more than tripled the total value of public land sales from 1816 to 1818.

The Bank of the United States contributed to popping the bubble in two ways. First, Jones ended the practice of redeeming the notes of one branch at another, which had drained specie from the Eastern branches to the Western branches, which had issued notes to fund the land speculation. Consequently, Western and Southern branches of the bank had to curtail their note issues, which functionally meant they could not create money to loan, thereby reducing credit. In addition, Jones insisted that the state banks resume redeeming their notes for specie, forcing the state banks to call in existing loans and to cut back on new lending. The results were dramatic: the Bank of the United States' specie reserves jumped from $2.5 million in 1819 to $3.4 million in January 1820. By spring 1821, specie reserves had more than doubled, to $8 million. Over roughly the same time, the bank's liabilities (i.e., money it had lent), dropped from $22 million in autumn 1818 to $10 million at the beginning of 1820, and the total value of circulating bank notes dropped by one-third over the same period.[31] Since the land bubble was fueled by easy credit and cheap money, the slowdown in lending popped the bubble; land prices dropped rapidly, as did the value of securities backed by land.

Meanwhile, under the terms of the Louisiana Purchase that President Thomas Jefferson negotiated in 1803, the United States was obligated to pay $4 million in interest on the bonds that the federal government had sold in 1803 to finance the purchase. In order to make this payment, the Bank of the United States, which was the federal government's fiscal agent, needed $4 million in specie, so it began redeeming state bank notes. Unfortunately, the state banks had issued far more notes than they had specie to cover, so they curtailed lending. In addition, most of the bonds were held by Europeans, meaning that the specie for the interest payment was being drained from the system, further weakening the economy. The resulting contraction, known as the Panic of 1819, resulted in a series of bank runs, business failures, and personal bankruptcies. It also led to a two-year recession and signaled that the United States had entered the modern business cycle.

Given the economic tumult occurring just as the bank came back into being, it became a lightning rod for people's dissatisfaction. Born out of necessity to face the economic crisis caused by the War of 1812, the Panic of 1819 convinced many Americans that the Bank of the United States was dangerous and ineffective. After all, far from preventing the panic, the bank's actions seemed to contribute to it and make the resulting depression worse. The economic downturn crystallized opposition to the bank and created its most powerful enemy: General Andrew Jackson, whose hatred of the Bank of the United States stemmed from losses he suffered due to the economic collapse.

2

The Era of
Good Feelings

While context is certainly important, the story of the Bank War demonstrates that agency—the decisions that individuals made—is equally so. Put another way, the Bank War did not just happen; it represents the sum total of various individuals' decisions made against a specific historical context. The Bank War's main antagonists, Andrew Jackson and Nicholas Biddle, represented two competing American values: democratic accountability and technocratic competence. Against a backdrop of expanding political opportunities for white males and a rapidly industrializing economy, conflict over the Bank of the United States was almost inevitable, but it was Jackson's ideological inflexibility and Biddle's political naïveté that moved events. At crucial moments in the drama, these individuals made choices that impacted the conflict's outcome. As one contemporary observer noted in December 1836, "If any man but Andrew Jackson had been at the head of the government, the Bank of the United States would still have been in existence."[1]

Andrew Jackson was born into a modest Scotch-Irish farming family in the Carolina backcountry in March 1767, the last of three children. His parents, Elizabeth Hutchinson and Andrew Jackson, had immigrated to the United States from Ireland only two years earlier, and young Andrew never knew his father, who was killed in an accident a few weeks before the future president's birth. When the American War for Independence began in 1775, Jackson, like his mother and two brothers, supported the Patriot cause. All three Jackson boys were involved in the war; the oldest, Hugh (born in 1763), died at the Battle of Stono Ferry in 1779, while Robert (born in 1764) and Andrew volunteered as couriers, carrying messages for the local militia. During the war, the British captured Robert and Andrew, and when a British officer demanded that Andrew clean the officer's boots, the defiant twelve-year-old refused. Enraged, the officer attacked Jackson with his sword, wounding the boy and fostering in Andrew a lifelong hatred of all things British. Andrew and Robert were eventually imprisoned for nearly two years. At the end of their captivity, the boys contracted smallpox. Released into their mother's care, Andrew eventually recovered but Robert died in spring 1781. Tragically, a few months later, Elizabeth died of cholera contracted while nursing prisoners aboard a British prison ship, leaving Andrew an orphan at age fourteen. For the rest of his life, Jackson blamed the British for these losses.

Needing to make his way in the world, the orphaned Jackson dabbled with saddle making and teaching before being admitted to the North Carolina bar in Jonesborough in 1787. In 1790, Jackson moved to the western edge of North Carolina into a territory that later became part of Tennessee. Jackson prospered as a frontier lawyer, and in 1788 he was appointed solicitor of the Western District. At about this time, he bought a 640-acre plantation he named the Hermitage. Starting with a workforce of nine slaves, Jackson eventually acquired approximately 150, most of whom grew and processed cotton.

The Hermitage, and its large slave population, made Jackson one of America's wealthiest men by the time he became president. His growing affluence and prominence in the community had guaranteed his selection as a delegate to Tennessee's 1796 constitutional convention. That same year, Jackson became the new state's single member of the US House, a position he resigned within a year. In 1798, Jackson was elected to the Tennessee Supreme Court, a position he held for six years, and in 1801, he was appointed commander of Tennessee's state militia.

In late 1812, simmering conflict between factions of the Creek Nation led to attacks on white settlements on the southeastern frontier. States across the South mobilized their militias, and Tennessee Governor Willie Blount ordered Jackson to take two thousand five hundred men and defeat the Creek. Setting out in mid-autumn, Jackson moved south, winning the Battles of Tallushatchee and Talladega that November. The following March, Jackson won a decisive victory at the Battle of Horseshoe Bend, where a force of two thousand six hundred Americans (both US Army and Tennessee militia) and six hundred Native Americans (Creek and Cherokees) routed a much smaller force of hostile Creeks, killing approximately eight hundred of the one thousand or so opposing force. In August, Jackson forced the Creeks to cede 23 million acres of land (now comprising parts of Alabama and Georgia) to the US government under the terms of the Treaty of Fort Jackson.

Jackson's greatest military success came in January 1815, at the Battle of New Orleans. The War of 1812 was a military disaster for the United States: less than two weeks after Jackson forced the Creeks to sign the Treaty of Fort Jackson, the British occupied Washington, DC, and burned down the White House. Though British and American negotiators in Ghent, Belgium, signed a treaty ending the war on December 24, 1814, that news did not reach the United States for a few weeks. Between Christmas Eve 1814 and January 8, 1815, Jackson repulsed British attempts to capture Louisiana and thereby force an end to the war in a series of engagements called the Battle of New Orleans, the best known and most celebrated battle of a war that was mostly an embarrassment for the United States. Commanding a ragtag force of five thousand militiamen, local volunteers, and Native Americans, Jackson inflicted a decisive defeat on the British that was the war's final major battle, cemented his reputation as a military hero, and paved the way for his presidential bid. Alexis de Tocqueville, who was no fan of Jackson's, credited the Battle of New Orleans for Old Hickory's election to the presidency. Writing in *Democracy in America*, de Tocqueville asserted that Jackson "was raised to the presidency, and has been maintained in that lofty station, solely by the recollection of a victory he gained, twenty years ago, under the walls of New Orleans."[2]

De Tocqueville was far from Jackson's only critic; Old Hickory's imperious behavior certainly brought him in for criticism that haunted him throughout his political career. In putting down an 1814 mutiny, Jackson did not prevent the execution of six militiamen who had been the mutiny's ringleaders, and following the Battle of New Orleans he had ordered the arrest of US District Judge Dominick Hall after Hall signed a writ of habeas corpus for a member of the Louisiana Legislature whom Jackson had arrested, demonstrating a penchant for ignoring the judiciary whenever it suited him. During the First Seminole War (1816–1819), Jackson invaded Spanish territory in Florida and summarily executed two British subjects who had been informing local Native Americans about his movements. His actions led many in President James Monroe's cabinet, including Secretary of War (and future Vice President) John C. Calhoun to call for Jackson's censure, which laid the groundwork for later conflict with the South Carolinian. In short, by 1820, Jackson had established a national reputation as a military hero but had also become the most polarizing figure of the so-called Era of Good Feelings.

Jackson's considerable political prominence was mirrored by his growing wealth. In 1794, Jackson and partner John Overton began speculating in land reserved by treaty to the Cherokees and Chickasaws. The following year, Jackson traveled to Philadelphia to sell fifty thousand acres of his own land and eighteen thousand acres owned by associate Joel Rice. Jackson sold the land for twenty cents an acre to Philadelphia merchant David Allison, who paid Jackson in promissory notes (financial instruments by which a buyer agrees to pay the seller a fixed amount at some future time). On returning to Tennessee, Jackson opened a trading post, purchasing supplies from Meeker, Cochran, and Company by transferring to them

Allison's promissory notes. Unfortunately for Jackson, Allison went bankrupt in 1797, and Meeker, Cochran informed him that he was now responsible for paying the amount due on Allison's notes.

Jackson was forced to barter his trading post for thirty-three thousand acres of land, which he then sold for twenty-five cents an acre to his friend, former territorial governor, and current US Senator William Blount (the half-brother of Willie Blount). Blount paid Jackson with a bank draft, but Jackson soon discovered that the draft was worthless because Blount's finances had been tied up with Allison's. Jackson was forced to take another promissory note from Allison, who died in debtor's prison shortly thereafter. Jackson sued Allison's estate and was eventually awarded five thousand acres in payment of the $20,000 owed to him. Jackson quickly sold the land at a loss and was doubly aggravated because the land that he had sold in 1795 to Allison for $10,000, and for which had never actually been paid, was now worth $200,000 and he was unable to recover it.

However, the story did not end there. In 1810, Jackson was mortified to learn that the judgment he had gotten against Allison's estate was invalid because the federal court had no jurisdiction over the matter (how Jackson, a lawyer and judge, did not know this at the time remains a mystery). Consequently, Jackson was not only legally liable for having sold the five thousand acres that he (apparently) did not legally own, but that liability was for the value of the land in 1810, which was much greater than the amount for which he had sold it. Jackson only managed to extricate himself from this precarious legal situation by releasing Allison's heirs from the balance of the $20,000 originally due him in exchange for clear title to the five thousand acres he had sold.

Nor was this Jackson's only run-in with banks. In 1818, the Bank of the United States' Nashville branch, where Jackson did much of his banking, refused to loan him money to prosecute his Seminole campaign. Three years later, the bank's New Orleans branch similarly denied his request for a loan, and he blamed financial reversals during the depression following the Panic of 1819 on the Bank of the United States. Consequently, in 1820, Jackson wrote to a friend, confessing, "You know my opinion as to the banks, that is, that the Constitution of our state, as well as the Constitution of the United States, prohibited the establishment of banks in any state."[3] At another point, he claimed, "I have always been opposed to the Bank of the u.s. [sic] as well as all state Banks of paper issues, upon constitutional grounds believing as I do, that the congress has no constitutional power to grant a charter and the states are prohibited from granting charters of paper issues."[4] Jackson supported a Tennessee law passed in 1827 that levied a tax on any bank that operated in the state but was chartered in another state. This was a pretty clear violation of the principle established by *McCulloch v. Maryland*, but it reflected Jackson's belief that paper money was unconstitutional. The lesson Jackson took away from this debacle was that specie was the only legitimate form of money and everything else was a fraud perpetrated by bankers against the common people of the country. Even biographer Robert Remini, who was generally sympathetic to Jackson, noted that Old Hickory "came to the presidency burdened with some pretty weird ideas about paper money."[5]

That Jackson had his eyes set on the presidency in 1824 was no secret. From a political perspective, it was the ideal time for him to run: President James Monroe had decided not to seek a third term, and he had no clearly identified successor (vice presidents did not typically succeed presidents in this era, and in any event, Daniel D. Tompkins's ill health prevented him from running), leaving the field wide open for the first time in American history. Since the turn of the nineteenth century, the country had more or less operated under a one-party system, and at least one newspaper, the *Boston Columbian Centinel*, described Monroe's administration as an "era of good feelings" characterized by political unity and declining partisanship. This description has been challenged by historians, but it is nonetheless true that the demise of the Federalist Party had muted (though not erased) partisanship in America during the late 1810s and early 1820s. Thus, the presidential election of 1824 was nominally a contest between four men of the same party—Senator Andrew Jackson, Secretary of State John Quincy Adams, Speaker of

Left to right, John Quincy Adams, Henry Clay, and William Crawford. (*Library of Congress*)

the House Henry Clay, and Treasury Secretary William Crawford—but the tensions and factionalism it exposed foreshadowed the emergence of a new party system.

Adams saw himself as the natural choice; the son of a president, Adams viewed the State Department as a stepping-stone to the White House (three of the previous five presidents—Jefferson, Madison, and Monroe—had served as secretary of state). Adams, who was fifty-seven in summer 1824, claimed more governmental experience than any other presidential aspirant, having served as US minister to Prussia, the Netherlands, Russia, and Great Britain, as well as having served a term as US senator from Massachusetts. Meanwhile, Crawford had a long and storied political career that involved at least two duels and stints in both the Georgia House of Representatives and the US Senate. In the latter capacity, Crawford served as the acting president pro tempore of the Senate following Vice President George Clinton's death in 1812. In 1813, President Madison appointed Crawford US minister to France, a position the Georgian held for two years until President Monroe appointed him secretary of war. Crawford served at the War Department for only a year, becoming secretary of the Treasury in 1816, a post he held for the remainder of Monroe's presidency.

Another strong contender was Clay, whose political power was considered second only to that of the president's. Born in Virginia, Clay had studied law with George Wythe, who had signed the

Declaration of Independence and mentored President Jefferson and US Chief Justice John Marshall. In 1797, Clay relocated to Lexington, where he practiced law and from where he was eventually elected to the US House. Amazingly, on his first day in the House, the other representatives elected Clay speaker, a position he held three times during his long political career. In the early 1810s, Clay was one of the most prominent war hawks, those advocating war with Great Britain. A committed nationalist, Clay was also the foremost advocate of the American System, a plan for industrial growth based on three connected elements: a protective tariff that would make American-made goods competitive with imports, federal subsidies for "internal improvements" (i.e., canals, roads, and railroads) to foster trade and communication, and a central bank. At forty-seven, he was one of America's best known and most important statesmen, one third of the Great Triumvirate that negotiated the Missouri Compromise of 1820.

Adams, Crawford, and Clay were all "insiders" and closely linked to the policies of the Monroe administration. By contrast, Jackson, though serving as senator from Tennessee, built his appeal on his status as an "outsider," a deft piece of political maneuvering for a sitting senator. Ironically, though Jackson thought of himself as a Jeffersonian, Thomas Jefferson did not share that belief. Writing in January 1825, while the House decided who would be inaugurated president, Jefferson noted:

> I feel much alarmed at the prospect of seeing General Jackson President. He is one of the most unfit men I know for such a place. He has had very little respect for laws or constitutions, and is, in fact an able military chief. His passions are terrible. When I was president of the Senate he was a Senator; and he could never speak on account of the rashness of his feelings. I have seen him attempt it repeatedly, and as often choke with rage. His passions are no doubt cooler now; he has been much tried since I knew him, but he is a dangerous man.[6]

The presidential election took place amid what one historian has called "the rise of American democracy," or a wave of expanding political rights for white males. In the fifteen years following the War of 1812, half of the states revised their constitutions or wrote new ones, and they all increased voting eligibility for white males by doing away with religious tests and property qualifications. Furthermore, many states changed the way their delegates in the Electoral College were selected, shifting toward popularly chosen electors. By the election of 1828, nearly all adult white males could vote in state and federal elections.[7] Despite this gathering tide of democracy, following a precedent that dated to 1796, an informal gathering of congressmen known as the Congressional Caucus met and nominated Crawford. The caucus represented a minority of congressmen, and the majority rejected its nominee for two reasons: they saw the nomination process as antidemocratic, and Crawford had suffered a debilitating stroke in 1823, though by the election his health had improved. The majority's failure to accept the caucus's nomination portended the breakdown of the Republicans' single-party control of the federal government and the arrival of a more democratic political age, forever changing the way candidates campaigned and presidents governed. Voting took on a strikingly sectional cast, with New England generally supporting Adams, and the mid-Atlantic, South, and parts of the West supporting Jackson. Jackson had a great deal of support in Pennsylvania. Biddle's close friend and relative by marriage, Thomas Cadwalader, supported Jackson, and Biddle even voted for Old Hickory. Ironically, given what was to come, Biddle voted for Jackson in 1824, though he later proudly boasted that during the election, "the name even of the Bank was never mentioned during the greatest political excitement."[8] Crawford did well in upper South along the Eastern Seaboard, and Clay's supporters were largely clustered in the West.

Jackson won the largest number of popular votes (41.4 percent), with Adams a distant second (30.9 percent). However, none of the candidates won a majority of the electoral votes, so, under the terms of the Twelfth Amendment, the contest moved to the House, which would award the presidency to one of the top three vote getters: Jackson, Adams, and Crawford. Because he had received the fourth-highest number of electoral votes, Clay was no longer a candidate but, as speaker of the House, he was in a position to exert a great deal of influence over the election's outcome. On a personal level, Clay detested Jackson, whom he saw as an uneducated savage prone to outrageous acts of violence, and on a political level, Adams's advocacy of internal improvements appealed to Clay. Consequently, Clay threw his support to Adams, who won the presidency on the first ballot.

Jackson and his supporters, who expected that the general would easily win in the House, were shocked and outraged, seeing the outcome as proof of corruption. This perception was further reinforced when Adams named Clay his secretary of state, a position widely viewed as a stepping-stone to the presidency. Jackson's supporters responded by damning what they called Adams's and Clay's "corrupt bargain"—the presidency for Adams in exchange for the State Department for Clay—and began planning to unseat Adams in 1828. Jackson also later claimed, though could never provide evidence to prove, that Crawford had used his position as secretary of the Treasury to influence the presidential election. Believing that the Bank of the United States had colluded with Crawford to deprive him of the presidency only reinforced Jackson's belief that it was corrupt and therefore its power needed to be curtailed. Writing to John C. Calhoun, Jackson asserted, "The whole exertions of the virtuous portion of the people will be required to put [the Bank] down."[9] Thus, Jackson's preexisting antipathy toward banks caused by his losses during the Panic of 1819 combined with a paranoid belief that the institution was out to get him, creating a witch's brew of anger and resentment that would decisively shape American politics and society for decades to come.

First, however, Jackson had to win the presidency, a goal he and his supporters set to achieving before the bunting from Adams's inaugural was removed from the Capitol. The presidential election of 1828 was vicious and bruising, a reflection of the Jacksonians' anger at what they considered Adams's fraud in having "stolen" the previous presidential election. Given Jackson and his supporters' belief that Adams and Clay were thoroughly corrupt, it should come as no surprise that the campaign was particularly nasty. Part of the campaign's viciousness can be attributed to two of Jackson's less attractive qualities: his tendency to take political attacks personally and his Manichaean belief that political differences were struggles between good and evil. Describing one political conflict to a friend, Jackson claimed, "I felt every virtuous spark in my system in a flame, and I stared villainy in the face, and lashed corruption."[10]

According to the Jacksonians, Adams was a degenerate who had purchased a billiard table for the White House (with government funds!) and a pimp who had secured a prostitute for the czar of Russia while serving as US minister there. The Adams people responded by digging up a long-dormant scandal in Jackson's closet having to do with his marriage. In 1791, Jackson married Rachel Donelson Robards, who believed that her first husband had divorced her and that she was therefore legally able to remarry. This was an error; no divorce had been granted, making Andrew and Rachel's marriage bigamous. Eventually, Rachel and her first husband were divorced, and she married Jackson (legally this time) in 1794. These events caused a minor scandal at the time, but that was nothing compared to the slander hurled at the Jacksons during the election of 1828, when one newspaperman rhetorically asked, "Ought a convicted adulteress and her paramour husband be placed in the highest offices of this free and Christian land?"[11] Rachel Jackson was largely shielded from these attacks because she spent most of her time at the Hermitage. Shortly after Jackson's victory, however, Rachel traveled to Nashville, where she heard the lurid stories circulating about her. A pious and fragile woman, the now elderly Rachel was shocked and dismayed by the rumors, which exacerbated her anxiety about becoming first lady of the United States. In short order, Rachel developed pleurisy and then suffered a fatal heart attack, which Jackson blamed on Adams and Clay. When the incumbent president sent Jackson a note about the transition, Old Hickory refused to respond or to call on Adams, who in turn refused to attend the inauguration. It was an inauspicious beginning to Jackson's administration and an indication of his penchant for making political issues personal.

During the election of 1828, Jackson's political advisers worked to keep the candidate out of public view, advising him not to respond to attacks or bind himself by making campaign promises.

Consequently, Jackson said little about banking, concerned that opposition to the Bank of the United States might cost him votes in Pennsylvania, a crucial state for any successful presidential campaign. What bound the Jacksonian coalition together was fealty to Jackson rather than any political agenda. In general, the Jacksonians opposed the Bank of the United States and high tariffs and supported hard money, but there were notable exceptions, so it was imperative not to alienate anyone. As a states' rights man, Jackson vehemently opposed Clay's American System and any federal spending on internal improvements, though his supporters in the West obfuscated the general's true views on this issue lest it cost him votes. The few statements Jackson did make were vague and allowed his audience to project their ideas onto the candidate.[12] As a result of these tactics and the general dissatisfaction with the incumbent, Jackson won a commanding 56 percent of the popular vote to Adams' 43.6 percent.

Biddle again voted for Jackson, though he was aware of Old Hickory's antipathy toward banks. According to Biddle's biographer, the Bank of the United States president did so "in the firm belief that, once in office, [Jackson] would be forced to change his opinion as Madison, Gallatin, Monroe, Rush, and other opponents of the national bank had done when serving as President of the United States or as Secretary of the Treasury."[13] In short, Biddle gambled that pragmatism would override Jackson's ideological aversion to the bank. As subsequent events demonstrated, Biddle had badly miscalculated, the first of many such mistakes that contributed to the Bank War.

Nicholas Biddle was born in Philadelphia on January 8, 1786, to a prominent Pennsylvania family whose roots went back to the state's founding. Nicholas's father, Charles, was vice president of the Supreme Executive Council of Pennsylvania (Benjamin Franklin was president), and the boy's uncle Edward served in the First Continental Congress in 1774. Among the Biddles' prominent acquaintances was US Vice President Aaron

Burr, who (while vice president) briefly stayed with the Biddles in Philadelphia after fleeing murder charges in New Jersey and New York arising from his fatal duel with Alexander Hamilton in 1804. Nicholas, who was one of ten children born to Charles and Hannah Biddle, was precocious, though of his early years, Biddle later recalled, "My boyhood was not I think happy."[14] Described by his biographer as "brilliant, impetuous, and daring," he was admitted to the University of Pennsylvania at age ten.[15] When the university refused to grant the teenager a degree, Biddle decamped to the College of New Jersey (later Princeton University), where, at fifteen, he graduated as the class valedictorian in 1801. In short, Biddle experienced a life of privilege far different from Jackson's.

Though the Biddles were Federalists, Nicholas had a strong belief in public service that transcended party politics. For instance, in 1804, Biddle accepted a position as secretary to US Minister to France John Armstrong. Armstrong was a Republican, and some of Biddle's friends accused him of abandoning his Federalist principles. However, as biographer Thomas Payne Govan noted, Biddle's father "had taught [Nicholas] that men could differ about politics and principles without descending to personal hatred, and too many friends of the Biddle family were Republicans to permit Nicholas to believe that association with members of that party was dangerous," a perspective wildly at odds with Jackson's.[16] From a very early age, Biddle demonstrated a commitment to nonpartisan public service and an unwillingness to turn political conflicts personal.

Biddle's position as Armstrong's secretary necessitated that the young man travel to Paris, which had a profound impact on his worldview. During his time in Europe, Biddle traveled extensively and cut his teeth assisting with an audit of the Louisiana Purchase as part of his work as Armstrong's secretary. In addition, he worked to settle American merchants' claims against the French government arising from the so-called Quasi-War, or the undeclared sea war between the two countries that raged between 1798 and 1800. Shortly thereafter, he traveled to London to take up his new job as secretary to US Minister to Great Britain James Monroe. In this position he impressed the future president, thus earning a powerful mentor and political patron and setting him on the road to the presidency of the Bank of the United States. Another lasting effect of Biddle's time in Europe was a solidification of his nationalist views. Biddle saw the Jefferson administration's foreign policy, which was based on keeping the United States neutral in the Napoleonic Wars, as flawed because it (in Biddle's view) communicated to Europe that the United States was weak. Consequently, Biddle became a lifelong advocate not only of a strong military but also of the American System and federally financed internal-improvement projects (usually transportation related). Later, he would come to see the Bank of the United States as the perfect instrument for achieving these nationalist goals.

In 1807, Biddle returned to Philadelphia, where he practiced law and wrote. It was during this period that Biddle began editing Meriwether Lewis and William Clark's report of their travels in the Louisiana Purchase territory, though he ultimately gave up the project in order to serve in the Pennsylvania House of Representatives. In 1812, Biddle began a brief stint as editor of *Port-Folio*, a well-known literary and political journal published in Philadelphia. In 1814, Biddle was elected to the Pennsylvania Senate, where his most important act was pushing for the Bank of the United States' recharter. Biddle's support for rechartering the bank distanced him from the Republicans with whom he had worked so closely over the preceding decade, but it also cemented his reputation as an authority on banking policy and paved his path to becoming president of the Second Bank of the United States in 1823.

For the time being, however, Biddle's political career hit a roadblock. The Republicans' dominance of national government meant that Federalists like Biddle were frequently unelectable. As a result, one of Pennsylvania's most powerful politicians, William J. Duane, opposed Biddle when the latter's name was floated as a potential candidate for the US House in 1816. Duane had immigrated to the United States from Ireland as a teenager, eventually becoming a lawyer in Philadelphia. In 1805, Duane married Benjamin Franklin's granddaughter and got himself elected to Pennsylvania's General Assembly. Duane saw himself as a Jeffersonian and opposed publicly financed internal improvements. After losing the election to the House in 1816, Biddle cast about for another outlet for his desire for public service. Only thirty-four at the time of his defeat, the Pennsylvanian made it a point to visit President Monroe regularly and frequently sent his former boss letters offering advice and encouragement, though seemingly with little success: the president did not immediately find a place for Biddle.

Circumstances turned in Biddle's favor the following year amid complaints about the administration of the Bank of the United States president, William Jones. Specifically, the pressure Jones had placed on the state banks to resume specie payments, even under the favorable terms offered by the bank, created a backlash and a credit contraction that threatened the economy. As a result, Jones reversed course, ordering the bank's branches to loan freely against the bank's stock, a move that enraged a group of stockholders led by Stephen Girard. The Philadelphia banker had opposed Jones's appointment in 1816 and now used the bank's unpopular policies to foment discontent against Jones. When the bank's stockholders ordered a general curtailment in loans at their meeting in July 1818, the resulting recession emboldened the bank's critics. Naturally, the bank's leadership instantly became targets of criticism, and Jones tried to reverse course by increasing the number of loans granted by the bank's Western branches, while his critics demanded that Congress investigate the bank and its seesawing lending policies.

Freshman Congressman John C. Spencer of New York succeeded in getting the House to pass, by an overwhelming majority, a resolution creating a committee to investigate the bank's operations. Spencer became the committee's chairman and convinced Biddle to serve as his unofficial adviser. Spencer's committee eventually uncovered evidence of mismanagement and fraud at the bank. The most serious infractions occurred in the bank's Baltimore branch, where it turned out that James A. Buchanan and James W. McCulloch, the branch's president and cashier, in collusion with other members of the staff, had formulated a conspiracy to use bank funds to make straw purchases of bank stock in order to increase their votes and thereby their influence over bank policy.[17] When they came up short of money, Buchanan and McCulloch arranged for the bank to loan them money, using the bank's own stock (which they valued at a 25 percent premium) as collateral. When they ran out of stock, they simply arranged for loans with no security. Eventually, they managed to secure over $3.5 million on stock loosely valued at less than $350,000. It was not until the bank audited the branches following the Panic of 1819 that Buchanan and McCulloch's "creative" financing came to light.[18]

McCulloch and Buchanan's fraud was just the worst outgrowth of Jones's hands-off approach to dealing with the bank's branches. The branches operated quite independently of the bank's headquarters in Philadelphia, which caused problems with regard to bank notes. The branches loaned money on their initiative without consulting Philadelphia, leading historian Edward S. Kaplan to call the management personnel of the Southern and Western branches "either incompetent or disobedient . . . [because] they paid more attention to local interests and concerns than to the directors in Philadelphia."[19] In fact, Jones was quite proud of the branches' independence, repeatedly refusing attempts to centralize control in Philadelphia, and many of the branches operated just like any other commercial bank.[20]

While Biddle was distressed at the clear evidence of fraud and mismanagement the committee discovered, he was nonetheless skeptical about Spencer's intentions. There were credible (though ultimately unfounded) rumors that Spencer was less interested in rooting out corruption for the sake of good government and more interested in using a scandal to promote New York Governor DeWitt Clinton's presidential aspirations. Trying to contain the political damage, Biddle pressed Spencer not to act rashly toward the bank, recommending that Congress tinker with, rather than replace, the institution. At the same time, Biddle wrote to Monroe, expressing the hope that Congress would be "wise enough to remedy the existing evils instead of increasing them, to reform the Bank instead of destroying it."[21]

Whether Biddle's advice swayed Monroe is unclear; at a minimum, Jones had to be replaced, and the president moved to effect that change. A faction of the bank's board of directors had allowed Jones to retain the bank's presidency during the House committee's investigation, but once its findings became public, Monroe used his authority to name directors pledged to electing a new president. Biddle's support for the Bank of the United States in the Pennsylvania General Assembly as well as his experience with international finance made him an obvious choice to serve on the institution's board, and in January 1819, President Monroe appointed Biddle. According to Biddle's biographer, "This appointment defined Biddle's career for the next twenty years. He who for so long had been seeking the proper employment of his talents in the service of the nation was at last named to a place for which he was fitted by nature, capacity, and training."[22] Biddle took his new position seriously, studying all of the available literature on banking and economics, quickly becoming what one biographer has termed the "Napoleon of finance."[23] What neither Biddle nor Monroe could have known in January 1819 was that this appointment would lead almost directly to one of the most important and far-reaching political controversies of the nineteenth century, a critical moment that shaped American politics and society for decades to come.

Seeing the writing on the wall, Jones resigned the bank's presidency in January 1819, and Stephen Girard used his influence to secure the unanimous election of former US House Speaker Langdon Cheves. This was surely a credit to Girard's political influence; most members of Monroe's inner circle distrusted and disliked Cheves, who had attacked the Madison administration while serving in Congress and had even opposed the bill chartering the bank in 1816. In an attempt to derail Cheves's ascension to the bank's presidency, Monroe even offered to nominate the former congressman to the Supreme Court, but Cheves demurred.[24] Described by one historian as, "Cold, self-confident, uncompromising, and courageous" and as a man who "had the essential qualities needed by a man whose duty it was to devise and carry through the severe and unpopular measures that would be required" to sustain the bank's credit, Cheves was elected bank president on March 6. In the interregnum between Jones's departure and Cheves's arrival, Biddle, who had been appointed to the bank's board January 1, essentially ran the bank.[25]

Cheves became the bank's president at a particularly dire moment in the institution's history. In addition to the scandal that led to Jones's resignation, the bank's finances were in shambles. The bank's specie reserves could barely cover its balances with Philadelphia's other banks, to say nothing of its bank notes in circulation. Worse, an interest payment on the Louisiana Purchase debt loomed, leading many to conclude that Cheves would be forced to suspend specie payments, an impression that did nothing to engender confidence that the bank's management had turned a corner. Cheves immediately took a number of drastic steps to quickly improve the bank's finances. He ordered branches in the West to stop issuing bank notes in order to slow the drain of specie caused by Western notes being redeemed at Eastern branches. He furthermore demanded $350,000 in specie from the Western branches and most of their share of the federal government's deposits in order to rebuild the Eastern branches' specie reserves and to pay the interest due on the Louisiana Purchase bonds. He dispatched an agent to London to secure loans to prop up the bank's finances, and he continued Jones's policy of reducing loans. Biddle, then functioning as the bank's de facto second in command, supported these policies, and even crowed to Treasury Secretary Crawford, "The Bank adopted its course with great deliberation, it adhered to it however painful the effort with great steadiness and it was rewarded with rapid and unequivocal success."[26]

Within four months, Cheves's policies had restored the bank's financial health, but success came at a high price: the bank's tight lending policies slowed the economy. In addition, by autumn 1819, Biddle and Cheves no longer saw eye-to-eye. While Biddle had supported Cheves tight-money policies earlier in the year, once the bank had regained its financial footing, the Pennsylvanian expected that the Western branches would again be allowed to issue notes, albeit with tighter controls. Cheves saw the matter differently, believing that allowing the Western branches to resume issuing notes would only cause the specie drain that had caused the bank's problems. In fact, Cheves envisioned a decentralized bank with largely autonomous branches responsible for issuing and redeeming their own notes against their own specie holdings. He firmly opposed having the bank provide a national currency and, with the backing of a majority of the bank's board of directors, petitioned Congress to amend the bank's charter by changing the law regarding the bank's notes. Under its charter, the bank's notes were to be accepted as payment to the federal government at face value anywhere, regardless of the branch that had issued the note. This was the entire purpose of paper currency, the goal of which was to create a stable, portable, and transferrable store of value. The problem was that it shifted the costs of transporting specie onto the currency issuer, which in this case was the bank. Since branches issued notes at their own discretion based on their own individual specie reserves, universal redemption raised the specter of draining specie from the branches in one region of the country to those of another.

Langdon Cheves. (*Library of Congress*)

In fact, Cheves went so far as to petition the secretary of the Treasury to change the bank's charter to allow the Treasury Department to discount the bank's notes when they were presented in places other than where they were originally issued. Such a change would cut the bank's expenses considerably; after all, it would not have to transfer specie between the branches that issued the notes and those that received them. However, universal redeemability at face value was a cornerstone of a national currency; changing the bank's charter in the way suggested by Cheves would make the institution no different from a state bank. When Congress balked at changing the bank's charter—after all, providing a national currency was one of the main reasons Congress chartered the bank in the first place—Cheves responded by maintaining the strict limits on note emissions, essentially abdicating the bank's responsibility to create a national currency. Worse, from an economic standpoint, Philadelphia ordered the branches to regularly redeem state bank notes and to avoid making loans that would require issuing Bank of the United States notes, further tightening the money supply in the middle of a depression. Biddle was so distressed by Cheves's policies that from late 1819 on, he looked with anticipation to December 1821, when his commission would expire and he could leave the bank.[27]

As luck would have it, Biddle was not the only member of the bank's board unhappy with his position. In late 1821, Cheves decided he would retire the following year, though he did not make his resignation public until the following summer, a few weeks before the triennial stockholders' meeting. Cheves hoped to be succeeded by Union Bank of Maryland President Thomas Ellicott. Ellicott had taken over the struggling Union Bank in 1819 during the panic that year and managed to keep the institution operating. But his bid for the Bank of the United States presidency was opposed by a number of influential stockholders, and he was never seriously considered for the position.[28] The dearth of candidates acceptable to the various factions on the bank's board caused a minicrisis. One of Biddle's friends wrote to the Philadelphian, lamenting, "Who will we have fore President of the Bank?"[29] Biddle's carefully written reply indicates that the Philadelphian had a suitable candidate in mind: himself.

Cheves did not want Biddle to succeed him. Biddle cautiously but actively campaigned for the job because he saw it as a stepping-stone for further advancement.[30] Biddle stopped at nothing to get President Monroe's and Treasury Secretary Crawford's endorsements. Given Biddle's closeness to Monroe going back to the president's days as minister to Great Britain, this was a small hurdle to jump, but it made all the difference. Once it became clear that Biddle had the administration's support, the race for the bank's presidency was essentially over. Even Cheves, who found Biddle a thorn in his side during the latter's term on the bank's board of directors, muted his opposition, and on November 25, 1822, Biddle was almost unanimously elected the bank's third president.

In a letter to Monroe, Biddle described the daunting challenges facing the bank's new president but asserted his belief that:

> The Bank is of vital importance to the finances of the govt. and an object of great interest to the community. That it has been perverted to selfish purposes cannot be doubted—that it may—& must—be renovated is equally certain. But they who undertake to reform abuses & particularity of that description must encounter much hostility and submit to much labor.[31]

Yet, despite these challenges, the presidency of the Bank of the United States had a number of features well suited to Biddle's temperament and ideals. For one thing, the incumbent was supposed to be nonpolitical, setting policy based on what was good for the country, not what was politically advantageous. In addition, given the bank's power and influence, the position offered the office holder the rare ability to effect real and lasting change.

One of the first things Biddle did on assuming the bank's presidency was increase liquidity and credit in an attempt to reenergize the economy. Under Biddle, the bank began making loans again, which increased the number of bank notes in circulation, and within six months, the effects were visible. From 1828 to 1832, the bank's outstanding loans swelled by nearly 30 percent, to $70.4 million, while the total value of notes in circulation increased more than fourfold.[32] Biddle authorized the branches to again issue notes and judiciously used its reserves to exercise "mild and gentle but efficient" control over the state banks' note issues, which ensured that those institutions did not overextend themselves. His long-term goal was to make the Bank of the United States the sole bank note issuer, creating a de facto national currency.[33] Biddle pursued this policy for social as well as economic reasons because he believed, "The best friends of the laboring classes are the banks; what laboring people want is labor, work, constant employment. How can they get it? In building shops and building houses; in coal mines; in making roads and canals; and now are all these carried on except by credit in the shape of loans from the banks. If it were not from such credits, nine-tenths of all works which give wages to labor would be at an end." Furthermore, he argued, "gold and silver are for the rich, safe bank notes are the democracy of currency."[34] This contradicted hard-money orthodoxy and points to one of the great ironies of the Bank War, namely, both Biddle and Jackson pursued their policies in the belief that those policies benefited the "common man."

Biddle reversed Cheves's decentralized structure by allowing directors who lived in cities with branches to attend those branches' meetings. While they could not vote, they nonetheless served as Biddle's eyes and ears and reminded the branches' directors that Biddle was watching. Summing up his philosophy, Biddle said, "My own theory of the administration of the Bank and my uniform practice, is to consider the Cashier of an Office, as a confidential officer of this Board, and to rely on him and to hold him responsible for the execution of [the Board's] orders."[35] All of these policies met with widespread public approval. In general, the state banks were happy with the Bank of the United States' increase in liquidity, and the value of its stock even increased, a reflection of the fact that it consistently turned a profit under Biddle's leadership. In fact, Biddle's presidency (up to the Bank War) was something of a golden age for the Bank of the United States. As David Kinley noted, during this period, "bank management was sound, government credit was excellent, the public debt was reduced, and the industrial and commercial situation was healthy."[36] Jackson biographer Robert Remini called Biddle "the best thing that ever happened to the Bank," while historian Edward Kaplan called the years between Biddle's assumption of the presidency and Jackson's election "the Bank's best years."[37]

However, the benefits of Biddle's credit expansion were not distributed equally. While the Boston and New York branches increased their loan origination by 80 percent during the first years of Biddle's tenure, the average for the bank as a whole was only 30 percent. Branches in the West did not expand their loans nearly as much as branches along the Eastern Seaboard, and some Western branches even decreased the number and amount of loans.[38] Biddle also refused to make long-term loans for the purpose of buying land or stock. Recent events had demonstrated to him the perils inherent in such loans, and he was loath to again have the bank contribute to a speculative bubble. Biddle's policies made him unpopular with some of the bank's stockholders, but he never lost sight of the fact that the bank was a unique institution that had responsibilities beyond those of an ordinary commercial bank. At one point he admonished a colleague who wanted to expand the bank's profitability by saying, "Let us not by hope of doing better or getting more business risk the prosperity and safety of the institution."[39]

For Biddle, part of protecting the bank's stability, and thereby fulfilling its responsibilities to the country, involved accumulating a capital surplus so it could weather sudden panics and other economic crises. When Biddle took over the bank, no such surplus existed, meaning the institution was vulnerable to sudden economic downturns. Over the course of Biddle's presidency, the bank built a $6 million surplus, but the opportunity cost was the lost profit that could have been generated on the surplus had it been invested. The surplus alienated some of the bank's stockholders, who perceived Biddle's conservative policies as missed opportunities for additional profit. During Biddle's presidency, the bank typically generated a 6 to 7 percent annual dividend. This was a decent return on investment, but hardly spectacular, leading some stockholders to complain that Biddle focused too intently on central banking to the exclusion of private profit.[40] These men were not shy about their unhappiness, and in 1823 one even went so far as to claim that "the only test of good banking is good dividends."[41] Statements like that reflected the state bankers' perspective on banking, but Biddle (whom historian Richard H. Timberlake Jr. described as "a stern but friendly shepherd of the commercial banks") saw things differently.[42] According to Biddle, "The State Banks may make as much money as they can without looking to consequences. But the Bank of the United States, while it makes money must take care always to keep itself in such an attitude that at a moment's warning, it may interpose to preserve the State banks and the country from sudden dangers."[43] Despite the generally positive relationships that the Bank of the United States had with the state banks during this period, there was always an underlying tension; like teenagers, the state banks appreciated the benefits that the bank provided but chafed under its control. Historian Walter B. Smith locates Biddle's problems in a simple fact: the bank attempted to supply "a 'sound currency' to a public that wanted sound money but did not want the consequences of policies necessary to make it sound."[44]

Some of the tension that underlay the state banks' relationship with the Bank of the United States was geographic. Though in Jacksonian America Philadelphia served as the country's banking and financial center, New York City's rapid growth during the first quarter of the nineteenth century meant that the Big Apple was poised to overtake the City of Brotherly Love. Much of that change can be attributed to the Erie Canal, a 363-mile man-made waterway across western New York State that lowered the cost of transporting goods between the Great Lakes and the Atlantic Ocean. Completed in 1825, the canal made it cheaper, easier, and faster to move raw materials from the US interior to the coast. But making New York City the canal's terminus ensured that the fruits of that growth would bypass Philadelphia. Naturally, this development created friction between the two cities, and that tension was exacerbated by what many New Yorkers perceived as Biddle's overly cautious monetary policies. As early as 1828, an anonymous stockholder warned Biddle about some New York bankers' jealousy over the fact that the Bank of the United States was headquartered in Philadelphia. According to the stockholder:

> You are doubtless aware of the opposition to your administration of the affairs of the Bank over which you preside, which has recently manifested itself in your City, New York and elsewhere. The Stockholders are under the impression that your object is to keep in check the State Banks and to regulate the Currency of the Country *at their cost*. This they say may not be inconvenient to you, while you receive the salary of the President of the Bank, but it does not suit them.[45]

In a letter to Biddle, Secretary of the Treasury Richard Rush claimed "the frog of Wall Street [New York] puffs himself into the ox of Lombard Street [Philadelphia], and will not have you abuse him."[46]

That geography was at least as important as actual policy is illustrated by the fact that, early in Jackson's presidency, New York Congressman Churchill Cambreleng reportedly said the bank could only be rechartered if its headquarters was moved to Manhattan.[47] During the fight over rechartering the bank in summer 1832, New Yorkers led the charge against the institution. For instance, one of the bank's most vociferous critics was *Albany Argus* editor Edwin Croswell. By far, however, the most important New Yorker was Martin Van Buren, a rising Empire State politico who vociferously opposed the bank because he saw it as an impediment to New York City's rise to financial leadership. Alexander Hamilton, son of Washington's Treasury secretary, described Van Buren (whom he knew personally) in a letter to Biddle as "an aspirant for the [presidency] ... [and] without principle, and totally destitute of sincerity." According to Hamilton, Van Buren "may smile and seem gracious, . . . [but] only to deceive."[48]

Van Buren played an important role in the Bank War. Born in Kinderhook, New York, in 1782, Van Buren was the first man elected president who was born after the United States declared its independence. His father, Abraham Van Buren, was a Jeffersonian Republican who was active in local politics and served for a decade as Kinderhook's town clerk. Martin received little formal education and began reading law at fourteen. In 1803, he was admitted to the New York State bar and soon became successful enough to pursue his real passion, which was politics. Allying himself with New York Governor George Clinton, Van Buren was rewarded with an appointment to Columbia County's probate court. In 1812, he was elected to the New York State Senate, and later he was the Empire State's attorney general. Van Buren supported both the War of 1812 and the Erie Canal, and his facility with arranging patronage appointments for his political allies and supporters won him the name the Little Magician. In 1821, he was appointed to the US Senate from New York, a position he held until winning that state's governorship in 1829. Van Buren served only a few weeks of his term, however, because in March 1829, Jackson appointed the New Yorker secretary of state.

By 1833, Van Buren was one of Jackson's closet political advisers and friends, dining with the president frequently and insinuating himself into Jackson's family. Having hitched his wagon to the incredibly popular Jackson, Van Buren wanted to ensure Old Hickory's political success (and, in so doing, pave the way for him to succeed Jackson in 1832 or 1836). In fact, Van Buren never seriously questioned the bank's constitutionality, conceding to one acquaintance, "I believe with Mr. Madison that the contemporaneous recognition of the Constitutional power to establish a bank by all departments of the government, and the concurrence of the people, has settled that question in favor of the power." Van Buren's opposition to the bank was first, last, and always rooted in the New Yorker's desire to see Manhattan eclipse Philadelphia as the US financial capital and thus strengthen his own political prospects.[49] Many of New York's bankers shared Van Buren's hostility toward the Bank of the United States. According to historian John M. McFaul, state bankers' attitudes toward it can be divided into three categories: indifference, support, and cautious hostility. This last response was mostly centered in New York and, to a lesser extent, Virginia, both of which preferred state regulations over those imposed by a national bank.[50] As a result, Van Buren was very sensitive to the optics of the Bank War, always trying to counter the (mostly correct) impression that his opposition to the bank was a largely geographic. At one point in summer 1834, Van Buren delicately turned down Jackson's request that the New Yorker come to see him, lest the public ascribe Jackson's policies to a "monied junto in N. York."[51] Biddle later described the Bank War as essentially a showdown between Philadelphia's "Chestnut Street and [New York's] Wall Street."

In addition to the stockholders' unhappiness with the bank's conservative lending policies and many New Yorkers' antagonism toward the bank, Biddle faced a backlash over his attempt to administer the bank in a nonpartisan way. As chapter 1 demonstrated, the composition of the bank's board of directors and its economic policies were always subject to political pressure, and in this sense Biddle's administration of the bank represented a departure from practice. From the outset, the Madison administration frequently made appointments to the bank's board for political reasons, and as the Era of Good Feelings came to an end, the intense partisanship of the emerging Second Party System only increased requests that Biddle find places for political allies and supporters. Biddle dealt with these requests as diplomatically as possible, responding in 1827 to a prominent New Yorker's request that he appoint some politically influential friends to the bank's board by noting, "I thank you for the suggestion in regard to the political character of the Board.

Martin Van Buren. (*National Park Service*)

These are considerations which tho' secondary are not to be overlooked and while I would not go out of the way to seek for the object among persons entirely equal in other respects, it would due weight."[52] Vague responses like these and Biddle's resistance to make appointments for political reasons could only stir up resentment and anger among those who believed that electoral success entitled them to use the bank to reward their friends and supporters.

Unhappiness with Biddle coalesced in an attempt to remove him from the bank's presidency in 1825, though the malcontents among the bank's stockholders were unable to secure a majority of votes in favor of their candidate. Two years later, Virginia Congressman Philip P. Barbour introduced a resolution in the House designed to force the federal government to divest itself of bank stock. Barbour said his goal was to destabilize the bank, but the resolution failed to pass, garnering only nine votes. Biddle saw Barbour's motion as a minor inconvenience that, having been defeated, only strengthened the bank's position. Writing after the motion was defeated, Biddle claimed:

> During the week of agitation which prevailed at the prospect of so large an amount of stock being thrown into the market, its price fell two or three per cent, but returned to its former rate as soon as the proposal was negatived. This measure was undoubtedly of an

unpleasant character, but in a large assembly, where every member is allowed to submit any motion, however ill-digested, the manner of treating it is the most important consideration & this has been favorable in the present instance so I am satisfied that the Bank gained much by the agitation of the question.[53]

Biddle's letter reflects two elements of his thinking that were to have profound implications for the Bank War: his disdain for the bank's critics and his faith in the institution's self-evident usefulness and power to protect it. Though Biddle dismissed expectations that the lopsided rejection of Barbour's motion "is decisive of the renewal of [the] charter," his letter nonetheless indicates a sense that congressional opponents were less existential threats to the bank and more like gnats to be swatted.[54] This attitude could result in punctilious and impolitic behavior, illustrated in the way he handled French spoliation claims. In 1831, the French agreed to pay 25 million francs in six annual installments to settle American claims arising from the Napoleonic Wars. However, the French government did not appropriate the money to pay the first installment, so when Secretary of the Treasury Louis McLane drew a draft on the French government through the bank, it essentially bounced. Adding injury to insult, Biddle charged the draft's principle, interest of 15 percent, and costs of protest and reexchange against the Treasury Department's accounts at the bank. Jackson reacted violently, decrying, "The want of punctuality in the French Government results in a penalty against the United States! This is the fidelity of [the bank] . . . this is the gratitude with which the government is requited."[55]

In another instance, Biddle betrayed his disdain for the bank's critics by cleverly circumventing the regulations Congress established for issuing bank notes. The Bank of the United States' recharter came during a period of considerable expansion in America's banking sector. In the twenty years after 1820, the number of state banks more than doubled, and the total value of state bank notes in circulation rose from approximately $41 million to $107 million. During these two decades, states frequently—some might even say recklessly—chartered banks in exchange for cheap loans or "bonuses" (i.e., large cash payments) from the new institutions. With regard to the state banks, the Bank of the United States exercised two levers—both having to do with paper money—that gave it enormous power over these institutions. The Bank of the United States accepted tax revenue paid in notes drawn on the state banks, which the bank—at its discretion—could decide to either hold or return to the state banks in exchange for specie. Since redeeming the state bank notes for specie drained those banks' specie reserves, the Bank of the United States could in effect curtail the state banks' loan origination and, with it, their profits.

One way Congress sought to protect state banks from competition with the Bank of the United States was to limit the number of notes the bank could issue by requiring that each note be signed by the bank's president and by the cashier of the branch issuing it. Biddle overcame this problem by having the bank issue drafts—essentially checks—that were issued in standard denominations and labeled as payable to the bearer. These drafts looked like notes and were accepted for tax payments. In this way, the bank managed to circumvent Congress's limitations on note issuance. This move was vintage Biddle: clever, pragmatic, and dismissive of congressional authority, an attitude that did much to create resentment among legislators who might otherwise have supported the bank in its confrontation with the Jackson administration.

Furthermore, despite congressional efforts to limit Biddle's power, the bank exercised an incredible amount of influence over the economy. By the time Jackson was inaugurated president in March 1829, the bank originated one out of every five bank loans in the nation and emitted approximately one-fifth of the country's bank notes. More impressive, the bank held one-third of the nation's specie reserves, making it the most important financial institution in the United States. As historian Arthur Fraas noted, "its operations touched virtually every aspect of the nation's economic life."[56]

One incident demonstrates the power Biddle had at his disposal. In 1826, Biddle used the bank's unrivaled financial position to obliterate Jacob Barker's financial empire. Barker was a colorful and well-connected New York financier. During the War of 1812, he had managed to secure a multimillion-dollar loan for the federal government and then founded the Exchange Bank of New York. After a brief stint in the New York Senate, Baker focused on expanding his banking interests, which he did throughout the early 1820s. The secret to Baker's success was leverage: He would purchase one bank and then use its resources to buy a controlling interest in a second bank. Once Baker controlled the second bank, he would have that bank loan him money (in the form of bank notes) to buy a third bank, and the process would start all over. In short, Baker's banks were each issuing notes against the same small supply of specie. This allowed him to purchase multiple banks quickly, but it had a potential flaw: as his banking empire grew, so did the number of bank notes those banks would have to redeem in specie. Seeing the potential for Baker's unchecked expansion to create a financial empire so large that its collapse would trigger a panic, Biddle redeemed the notes issued by Baker's various banks. Because these bank's had issued notes with little actual specie to back them, redeeming a large number of them at once created a forceful wind that toppled Baker's economic house of cards.

On the one hand, actions like this helped cleanse the banking sector of bad actors and make it more secure. That a steadying force was required is unquestionable. The state banks' specie reserves were almost uniformly insufficient to cover even modest note redemptions, despite the fact that states frequently penalized banks who suspended specie redemptions by charging them 12 percent interest on any unredeemed note.[57] On the other hand, Biddle's actions (and his arrogance) coupled with the bank's size and unrivaled power also made it a target of criticism. In addition, the growing partisanship caused by the breakdown of the Era of Good Feelings contributed to a desire to find political wedge issues that candidates could use to generate enthusiasm in an increasingly democratic political environment. Thus, when Andrew Jackson became president in March 1829, all of the pieces—Biddle's arrogance, the bank's power, Jackson's ideological antipathy toward banks, the partisan nature of the increasingly democratic American political system—were in place for an epic showdown between the new administration and the Bank of the United States.

3

Scandals, Vetoes, and a Looming Crisis

The conflict over the Bank of the United States during Jackson's presidency can essentially be divided into two periods: the calm before the storm during most of Old Hickory's first term and the period of all out war beginning in 1832. Though there were certainly skirmishes between 1829 and 1832, in general, Biddle did his utmost to appease the new president and work with the administration to assuage Jackson's concerns about the bank. As this and the last chapter make clear, however, Biddle's efforts were futile; Jackson was ideologically opposed to the Bank of the United States, and there was simply no way to reconcile his beliefs with the bank's continued existence. It was only a series of political crises, aggravated by Jackson's personality and style, that prevented the president from moving aggressively against the bank during his first term. Finally, the inchoate nature of the Democratic Party during Jackson's first term militated against strong action against the bank;

there were simply too many people in the party who, unlike Jackson, recognized its utility and value. That it took Biddle so long to realize this is a function of the fact that Jackson intentionally sent the Pennsylvanian mixed messages about the administration's intentions. In short, the Bank War is the ideal case study of national politics in the so-called Age of Jackson, and any history of the conflict between Biddle and Jackson over the bank's recharter is necessarily a history of Jackson's administration as a whole.

Inaugurated president a few days shy of his sixty-second birthday, Jackson was in bad shape. Bullets remained lodged in his body from his many duels, causing him to frequently cough up blood. At six-foot-one and 140 pounds, Jackson looked as though he was in danger of blowing away, and throughout his time in the White House, he suffered from a panoply of discomfort that included debilitating headaches and stomachaches and recurrent dysentery. These were treated with medicines that contained lead and mercury, almost surely exacerbating his medical problems and increasing his pain.[1] Nevertheless, for the next eight years, Jackson never shrank from conflict, seeing political battles as fights to the death that he was always determined to win.

US Chief Justice John Marshall administered the presidential oath of office to Jackson on Wednesday, March 4, 1829. There is more than a little irony in the fact that Marshall, who wrote the Supreme Court's majority decisions in *Marbury v. Madison* (which established the principle of judicial review) and *McCulloch v. Maryland*, was the one who administered the oath to Jackson, because Old Hickory opposed the decisions in both of those cases. In fact, during his presidency, Jackson attacked the principle of judicial review established in *Marbury* v. *Madison*, one of the most consequential decisions to come of the Marshall court. Following the inauguration, Jackson rode a white horse back to the Executive Mansion and hosted a public reception that quickly degenerated into a drunken melee. The new president was nearly crushed to death by the surging throngs, and in the general confusion, several thousand dollars worth of White House china was destroyed, leading Supreme Court Justice Joseph Story (who disliked Jackson and opposed Jacksonianism) to claim that "the reign of King Mob seemed triumphant." It was a fitting beginning to Jackson's controversial and precedent-shattering presidency.

At this stage, Biddle did not yet recognize the threat that Jackson posed to the bank. In a letter to a friend shortly after the election, Biddle confidently reported, "I do not incline to fear anything for the Bank from the change of Administration." He even went so far as to suggest, "When we see who is to be our new Secty of the Treasy, we can seriously consider the application for a renewal [of the bank's charter]."[2] Between Jackson's inauguration and January 1832, Biddle tried to appease the new president. Many observers were not nearly as sanguine about the bank's prospects under a Jackson presidency. Businessman Roswell L. Colt, president of the Society for Establishing Useful Manufactures, reported to Biddle that one of their mutual acquaintances advised him to sell his shares of stock in the bank because of the incoming president's hostility to it.[3]

These dire warnings were belied by the fact that Jackson quickly appointed a cabinet that seemed favorably disposed to the Bank of the United States. This may seem strange, given Jackson's long-standing antipathy toward the bank, but their appointments were necessitated by the diverse and inchoate nature of the Jacksonian coalition. For instance, Secretary of War John Eaton and Jackson's friends William B. Lewis and John Overton all supported the bank. Overton even served on the Nashville branch's board of directors. In addition, prominent Pennsylvania Jacksonians supported the bank, as did James A. Hamilton (son of Alexander Hamilton, who had established the bank's predecessor) and former US senator from Delaware (and future secretary of the treasury) William McLane. Meanwhile, other prominent Jacksonians, including US Senator Thomas Hart Benton of Missouri and journalist Amos Kendall, vociferously opposed the bank and counseled Jackson to take immediate action against it.[4] Therefore, it was extremely hard for Biddle to predict or prepare for the administration's actions.

Though Jackson's actions toward the bank in the early days of his presidency were ambiguous and contradictory, his underlying aversion to it was exacerbated by rumors that some branch directors had used the institution's resources to support Adams's reelection bid. Jackson believed these rumors, at one point complaining to his former partner Overton about "the injurious effect . . . the directors of the Bank had in our late election which if not *curbed* must destroy the purity of the right of suffrage."[5] These rumors ran directly counter to the scrupulous neutrality that Biddle pursued as president of the bank and were ironic given the fact that Biddle voted for Jackson in 1824 and 1828. Responding to these rumors, Biddle noted on December 29, 1828:

> You ask "whether any of the branches, in any way whatever, except the individual votes of the Directors, interfered in the late contest." Most certainly not—in the slightest degree. There is no one principle better understood by every officer in the Bank, than that, he must abstain from politics, and I have not seen nor heard of any one of them in any part of the Union, who has been engaged in this controversy. . . . We believe that the prosperity of the Bank & its usefulness to the country depend on its being entirely free from the control of the Officers of the Gov., a control fatal to every Bank, which it ever influenced. In order to preserve that independence it must never connect itself with any administration—& never become a partisan of any set of politicians. . . . [W]e say with equal truth, that the Bank is neither Jackson man not an Adams man, it is only a Bank.[6]

Two years later, Biddle reiterated the point, saying to Republican newspaperman Joseph Gales, publisher of the *National Intelligencer*, "the Bank has sense enough to be neither for Adams nor Jackson but for the country and sound currency."[7] During the height of the showdown over recharter in summer 1832, Biddle claimed, "They, who administer the Bank, administer it for the country, not for any party, and although denounced by these persons in power, instead of avenging themselves, have striven . . . to avert every inconvenience from these measures with quite as much zeal as if they or their friends were authors of them."[8]

Statements like these demonstrated Biddle's aversion to partisanship, an attitude that contributed to his conflict with the Jackson administration. At one point, Biddle noted in disgust, "The violence of party . . . disgraces our country."9 Biddle later claimed that he intended to forge an independent course "in direct opposition, if need be, to the personal interests and wishes of the President and every officer of the government."10 This was a break with past practice; as the two previous chapters made clear, the Bank War, from its inception, was caught up in a web of political intrigue. That being said, Biddle was hardly the only American banker who eschewed political attachments; historian John McFaul has concluded that "the safest conclusion about banking interests during the Jacksonian era is that state banks were reluctant to inject themselves and their institutions into politics."11

Ironically, Jacksonian era bankers' aversion to politics actually contributed to the Bank War, for two reasons. First, Biddle's refusal to turn the Bank of the United States into a patronage engine for the administration contributed to the president's ire toward the bank. Second, it was this nonpartisan independence that did so much to put him at odds with the Jackson administration. Put simply, nonpartisanship was out of style in Jacksonian America. Former New York Mayor Philip Hone, an anti-Jacksonian businessman, lamented this change in 1839, saying, "The public good! Fudge! What does it mean? The term is often used for purposes of humbug, but its meaning is obsolete."12

One of the reasons Hone felt this way was that the spoils system, so called because of Jacksonian Senator William L. Marcy's infamous declaration "to the victor go the spoils," was a cornerstone of Jacksonianism. Basically, "spoils" in the form of government jobs (patronage) and contracts were awarded to individuals based not on merit but on the strength of their support for the winning candidate. The spoils system reflected the Jacksonians' belief that any individual of average intelligence and capacity could adequately discharge the duties of any government office. Up until Jackson's presidency, transfers of power from one administration to the next had led to little upheaval in government employment. In general, this reflected the Founding Fathers' dislike of parties and the fact that, since 1800, the federal government had been more or less controlled by a single party. During the 1828 presidential campaign, however, Jackson's friends promised to distribute government jobs and contracts to his supporters. When he became president in 1829, Jackson made good on these promises, removing approximately 10 percent of incumbent officeholders.

Given that Jacksonianism did not represent a coherent political ideology with a defined set of commonly held beliefs, something else had to be found to unite the diverse members and ensure party discipline. Patronage became the glue that held together the emerging Democratic Party, described by Martin Van Buren as an unlikely coalition of "the planters of the South and the plain Republicans of the north."[13] The reliance on patronage reflected the fact that despite Jackson's commanding victory in the 1828 presidential election, the Tennessean remained weak politically due to the inchoate nature of American politics. On paper, Jackson could count on large majorities in the House (177 to 136) and the Senate (26 to 22), but as Van Buren noted, many of these were not "very deeply imbued in the [party's] principles."[14] Given the widely divergent interests of the party's various factions, the Democrats were riven by a variety of tensions and contradictions, and without the spoils system, the Democrats could not have won five of the seven presidential contests from 1828 to 1856.

Reflecting on the Bank War later, Biddle decided that it was motivated by the Jacksonians' desire to turn the Bank of the United States into a patronage engine, and there is good evidence to support this conclusion. Writing in 1833 to Thomas Cooper, the president of South Carolina College and a professor of political economics, Biddle claimed:

"[S]oon after [Jackson and his supporters] came to power, there was a deliberation in the Caucus of the most active of the Jackson party as to the means of sustaining themselves in place—and the possession of the Bank was ranked as a primary object. For this purpose they began in 1829 with an effort to remove an obnoxious President of one of the Branches—which was to be followed by a systematic substitution of their creatures throughout the whole institution. This experiment failed, owing to the firmness of the

President Andrew Jackson, left, illustrated shortly after his first inauguration in 1829. (*Library of Congress*) Nicholas Biddle, right, with the Second Bank of the United States in the background. (*Pennsylvania Historical and Museum Commission*)

Directors who determined that they would not permit the interferences of the Executive Officers. . . . From that moment on they despaired of turning the Bank to their political purposes, and have been intent on breaking it down to substitute some machinery more flexible.[15]

Though Biddle offered no proof for his assertions, the fact that at least some Jacksonians viewed the bank as a source of political rewards can be inferred from Treasury Secretary Samuel Ingham's unsolicited statement to Biddle in July 1829 that the new administration in no way desired "to derive political aid from the Bank."[16] In one instance, Postmaster General John McLean (whom Jackson would soon appoint to the Supreme Court) wrote to Biddle about rumors that the directors of the bank's branches in Louisville and Lexington had refused to loan money to prominent Jackson supporters and had used their influence to help Adams' supporters. Revealing his real concern—that of securing federal spoils—McLean urged Biddle to select branch directors who were favorable to Jackson, hinting at the consequences for failing to do so. "Being friendly to the Bank myself," he wrote, "I should regret to see a political crusade got up against it. Some, I know, are ready to engage in this course."[17]

Biddle either did not get the hint or chose to ignore it. In his response to McLean, Biddle assured the postmaster general that after investigating the matter, he was convinced that (except in one instance) the branch directors had not "intermeddled with politics."[18] He noted:

> The truth is, that almost all the misfortunes of the Bank of the United States are traceable, directly or indirectly, to politics. In Kentucky, the losses [to the bank from unpaid loans] were in great measure incurred by politicians of all sides whose influence procured them undue facilities which ended, as frequently happens, in such cases by running them as well as crippling the Branches. These things have made us sensitive on that point, & unwilling to see any great political influence introduced, which might lead to a recurrence of similar misfortunes.[19]

Biddle's response neatly encapsulated his core belief that the bank should remain nonpartisan, if for no other reason than self-preservation, but it also demonstrated his political naïveté, and Jacksonian complaints about the bank's interference in the presidential election did not go away.

A few months later, New Hampshire Senator Levi Woodbury complained to Biddle about the bank's Portsmouth branch. That branch was managed by Jeremiah Mason, a close friend of Massachusetts Senator Daniel Webster's, who had vigorously campaigned against Jackson in 1828. At one point, prominent New Hampshire Jacksonian Isaac Hill (soon to be appointed second comptroller of the currency) had complained to Mason, "The friends of General Jackson in New Hampshire have had but too much reason to complain."[20] The complaints against Mason were transparently partisan, and Biddle was inclined to dismiss them. However, Woodbury had also shared his concerns with Jackson's secretary of the Treasury, Samuel Ingham, who was personally and politically close to Vice President Calhoun. As Calhoun had vigorously supported the bank's charter in 1816, Ingham's letter to

Biddle asking the bank president to look into Woodbury's complaints took on added importance. In order to mollify the administration, Biddle took some steps toward increasing loans to Jackson's supporters, though certainly not to the degree that Ingham had hoped. Biddle's investigation amounted to asking the employees of the branches involved to look into the complaints and write a report; it concluded that the charges against Mason were "a very small intrigue to supplant an honest & efficient officer, who was of course continued in his place."[21]

The situation got more complicated when Biddle received a letter from Comptroller of the Currency Isaac Hill, who was politically close to Jackson. Hill admitted spreading the rumors about Mason because the branch director had failed to loan money to prominent Jackson supporters in New Hampshire. Hill's admission enraged Biddle, who vented his spleen in a letter to Ingham and later exonerated Mason of any wrongdoing. For his part, Ingham interpreted Biddle's rage as an attempt to sweep the whole matter under the rug, noting that he objected to "a course of action which either resists inquiry, or, what is of the same tendency, *enters upon it with a full persuasion that it is not called for.*"[22]

Furthermore, according to Biddle, the bank answered "to Congress, and to Congress alone. . . . [N]o Executive officer of the Government, from the President of the United States downward, has the slightest authority to interfere" with the institution's management. Foreshadowing later events, Ingham retorted that the bank of the United States was, in fact, subordinate to federal authority, reminding Biddle that the Treasury secretary had the authority to remove the federal government's deposits from the institution at any time.[23]

The administration struck back at the bank when Secretary of War John Eaton notified Mason that the Portsmouth branch would no longer process pension payments for veterans of the War for Independence. Eaton requested that Mason forward all records and funds related to the pensions to the bank's Concord branch. Mason in turn passed the request along to Biddle and asked for instructions. Biddle directed Mason to refuse Eaton's request on the grounds that it was not legal. Clearly, relations with the new administration were not ideal, but Biddle vowed "not to give way an inch in what concerns the independence of the Bank, to please all Administrations past, present or future."[24]

This was bold talk, but the reality was far more complicated. While Biddle jealously guarded the bank's independence, he was nonetheless willing to try to appease the president. For instance, Biddle engineered the appointment of directors at various branches, including New York, Baltimore, Portsmouth, and New Orleans who were friendly to or connected with the new administration. Biddle also dispatched various bank personnel to meet with Jackson in order to convince him that the institution was not hostile to the administration. There is little evidence that these efforts influenced Jackson's attitude toward the bank.[25]

Biddle even went so far as to devise a scheme for paying off the national debt, a move that was dear to Jackson's heart. By the late 1810s, the federal government was actively retiring the US national debt. Except for 1821, America's national debt decreased every year from 1817 to 1835, with approximately 40 percent of the federal budget earmarked to meet this goal.[26] Though some looked on the prospect of a debt-free America as a blessing (Jackson later referred to the national debt as "the wasting canker of the nation"), Biddle saw things differently. Once the debt was retired, the government would come under enormous pressure to lower the tariff, thereby injecting massive liquidity into the economy. In 1830, Jackson himself noted that once the debt was paid, it was unlikely Congress would lower the tariff, so the surplus should be reapportioned to the states based on their representation in Congress (a formula that, incidentally, privileged slave states, whose representation was artificially inflated by the practice of counting slaves as three-fifths of a person for the purpose of apportioning congressional representation).[27] Biddle and others feared that the abundance of cheap money would contribute to a speculative bubble like the one that had led to the Panic of 1819. Instead, Biddle advocated spending public money on internal improvements, and in autumn 1824, he helped organize the Pennsylvania Society for the Promotion of Internal

Improvements. Nevertheless, under a plan Biddle sketched to Jackson in 1829, the federal government would sell its shares of bank stock and authorize the bank to take on the national debt in lieu of a bonus for recharter. In so doing, Jackson could achieve his dream of paying off the national debt in a single term, thereby accomplishing one of his most ambitious goals. In a meeting with Biddle, Jackson even thanked the bank president for the plan, saying he might even consider submitting it to Congress, but nothing ever came of Biddle's proposal.[28]

Biddle's attempts to appease Jackson reflected the Pennsylvanian's erroneous assumptions about the nature of the opposition to the bank. In short, Biddle believed that the bank was a positive influence on the American economy and therefore opposition to it resulted from ignorance or misunderstanding, both of which could be overcome simply by educating the public. As he noted in an 1831 letter to journalist Joseph Gales, Biddle believed "that nine tenths of the errors of men arise from their ignorance— and that the great security of all our institutions is in the power, the irresistible power, of truth."[29] It never occurred to Biddle that the very reasons he believed the bank was a positive good might strike people as intimidating and antidemocratic. Maryland Attorney General Roger B. Taney, who was to play a crucial role in the drama over the bank, aptly described the Jacksonians' fears about the Bank of the United States' antidemocratic potential when he argued in 1849, "The Bank was undoubtedly capable of exercising great influence and possessed power with which no corporation can be safely trusted in a republican government."[30]

Though Jackson came into office with a passionate hatred of the bank, he did not have a plan for what, if anything, should replace it. Shortly after his inauguration, he asked former Tennessee Representative Felix Grundy to develop a plan for remedying the Jacksonians' constitutional objections to the bank. Grundy was an excellent choice for this task, given that he had put forward, and then withdrawn, a motion in the House to study the feasibility and desirability of chartering a central bank during the War of 1812. Delivered in mid-October, Grundy's plan called for the charter of a national bank headquartered in Philadelphia with branches in all of the states. However, unlike with the Bank of the United States, there would be no stockholders; instead, Congress would elect the bank's directors, and the branches' profits would fund internal improvements in their respective states. In addition, the states would control the branches, though this provision concerned Jackson; the president feared that during a war, the states "might frustrate a campaign or sacrifice an army upon some frivolous pretext for refusing the payment of Treasury drafts."[31]

On the one hand, Jackson found much to admire in Grundy's plan and forwarded it to Treasury Secretary Ingham. On the other hand, the president seemed unable to articulate what he wanted to replace the bank, vacillating between reforming the institution and creating something new. As historian Donald B. Cole aptly described the situation, "Uncertain in his own mind, he appeared resigned to several years of discussions about a new bank."[32] Meanwhile, despite the lack of a clear-cut alternative, Van Buren convened a meeting of Jacksonians in Richmond to plot strategy for destroying the bank. Van Buren urged caution, noting that public opinion had shifted in the bank's favor. The New Yorker noted that the Jacksonians would have to proceed carefully and build a case against the bank lest they end up on the wrong side of public opinion.[33]

When Jackson presented Grundy's plan to Congress, it foundered. Though the House Ways and Means Committee reported its belief that the plan "proceeded from the most disinterested patriotism, and was exclusively designed to promote the welfare of the country," it nonetheless condemned the proposal. In a more telling admission, Maryland Senator Samuel Smith, a well-known Jacksonian, described the president's proposal in a letter to Biddle as "such a system of power and patronage" and noted that, had former President John Quincy Adams proposed such a program, "what a noise and out-cry we democrats would have made."[34] Smith's statement reinforces the conclusion that on some level, the administration's war on the bank had less to do with constitutional scruples and more to do with control over patronage, which did nothing to help Grundy's plan in Congress.

Jackson clearly realized that congressional opinion was not on his side, so he began a concerted effort to arouse public hostility to the bank. Jackson was infuriated by the fact that his friend Duff Green, publisher of the *United States Telegraph*, had not publicly attacked the bank, at one point raging that Green's "idol," Vice President Calhoun, "controls him as much as the shewman does his puppits, and we must get another organ to announce the policy, and defend the administration."[35] Jackson's statement is a marker of just how bad the war between Van Buren's and Calhoun's supporters had become. In October that year, Francis P. Blair (with extravagant promises of government printing contracts) established a new paper in Washington, the *Globe*, which was explicitly designed to be the administration's propaganda organ. Blair was born in Virginia in 1791, but he moved to Kentucky, where he graduated from Transylvania University in 1811. The sickly and frail Blair had contributed to Amos Kendall's *Argus of Western America*, and his strident opposition to nullification and to the Bank of the United States recommended him to Jackson. In fact, Jackson and Blair became fast friends, and the newspaperman even accompanied the president on vacation, and Old Hickory ensured that the *Globe* received the lion's share of executive branch patronage. As a result, Jackson could count on Blair to slavishly disseminate the president's views.

Even with the *Globe* acting as Jackson's mouthpiece, the president and his cabinet sent mixed signals about the administration's intentions, a reflection of the inchoate nature of the party and the diversity of opinion on the bank in the cabinet. Less than a month after Van Buren's meeting in Richmond, Biddle met with the president to discuss the bank's future. During their meeting, Jackson "expressed himself in the most clear and decided manner friendly to the Bank . . . calling it a blessing to the country . . . [and expressing] a high regard for its excellent president," according to one visitor. The president downplayed his antipathy toward the bank, mentioning only that he had some constitutional quibbles about the institutions but declaring himself "perfectly satisfied" with Biddle's management of the institution.[36] According to Biddle's notes of the meeting, Jackson said, "I do not dislike your Bank any more than all banks. But since I read the history of the South Sea Buddle, I have been afraid of banks."[37] Though the president did say, "I think it right to be perfectly frank with you . . . I have read the opinion of John Marshall [in *McCulloch v. Maryland*] who I believe was a great and pure mind, and could not agree with him, though if he had said that as it was necessary for the purpose of the national government there ought to be a national bank I should have been disposed to concur; but I do not think that Congress has a right to create a corporation out of the ten mile square [of the capital]," the general tenor of their discussion was friendly.[38] Jackson's statements to Biddle were totally disingenuous, as later events showed, and reflected another unattractive feature of the president's character: his willingness and ability to use deceit to keep his political opponents off-balance. As one of Jackson's earliest biographers observed, the president "was capable of the profoundest dissimulation," and nowhere was this tendency toward dishonesty more evident than in Jackson's course during the Bank War.[39] In fact, the mixed signals Jackson and other members of the administration sent to Biddle about the president's intentions toward the bank contributed to Biddle's confusion about it and made conflict over its recharter more, rather than less, likely.

Jackson's conciliatory statements to Biddle are belied by a conversation the president had later that month. At the end of November, Jackson had a breakfast meeting with James A. Hamilton, son of former Treasury Secretary Alexander Hamilton. Jackson showed Hamilton a draft of his upcoming annual message (a precursor to the State of the Union address) and asked Hamilton to edit the message. Hamilton did so that evening and the following morning returned to the White House. To Jackson's surprise, Hamilton had excised the president's harsh criticism of the bank, leaving only a brief and temperate statement that read:

> The charter of the Bank of the United States expires in 1836, and its stock holders will most probably apply for a renewal of their privileges. In order to avoid the evil resulting from precipitancy in a measure involving such important principles and such deep pecuniary interests, I feel that I can not, in justice to the parties

interested, too soon present it to the deliberate consideration of the Legislature and the people. Both the constitutionality and the expediency of the law creating the bank are well questioned by a large portion of our fellow citizens, and it must be admitted by all that [the bank] has failed in the great end of establishing a uniform and sound currency. Under these circumstances, if such an institution is deemed essential to the fiscal operations of the Government, I submit to the wisdom of the Legislature whether a national one, founded upon the credit on the Government and its revenues, might not be devised which would avoid all constitutional difficulties and at the same time secure all the advantages to the Government and country that we expected to result from the present bank.[40]

Jackson asked Hamilton, "Do you think that is all I ought to say?" When Hamilton affirmed that it was best to say little about the bank lest the president stir up unnecessary political opposition, Jackson laughed and replied, "My friend, I am pledged against the bank, but if you think that is enough, so let it be."[41]

James Hamilton's brother, Alexander Jr., warned Biddle that Jackson planned to criticize the bank in his annual message, but Biddle—believing the president's solicitude during their meeting in November indicated that Jackson could be appeased—did not believe him.[42] As a result, Biddle was blindsided by Jackson's assertion that the bank's constitutionality and expediency were open to question. Clearly, Jackson had lied to the banker. In a letter to a friend, Biddle complained, "It is scarcely three weeks, since [Jackson] expressed to me in person the greatest confidence in the administration of the Bank and his determination to make public acknowledgment of its services in paying off the debt, nor was there given any intimation of his purpose to speak of it thus."[43]

Nevertheless, Biddle seemed loath to admit that he had been hoodwinked by the wily president or that the bank's future was in jeopardy. A few days after Jackson released the annual message, Biddle wrote to Alexander Hamilton Jr., noting:

> My impression is that these opinions expressed by the President are entirely & exclusively his own, and that they should be treated

as the honest tho' erroneous notion of one who intends well. We have never had any idea of applying to Congress for a renewal of the charter at the present session—and of course should abstain from doing so now. Our whole system of conduct is one of abstinence and self defense.

If Biddle placed his confidence in Jackson's good intentions, the President placed his in the American people to follow where he led. On December 19, Jackson mentioned to James Hamilton that having raised questions about the bank's usefulness and constitutionality, he "had confidence that [the voters] would do their duty."[44]

Nowhere was the Jacksonian coalition's diversity and factionalism on greater display than in Congress' response to Jackson's complaints about the bank. Many in both Congress and the president's cabinet did not share Jackson's concerns about the bank's constitutionality or its alleged failures to provide a national currency. As late as December 1830, six senators and fifty congressmen—otherwise all good Jacksonians—supported rechartering the bank, while Pennsylvania's Jacksonians generally supported the institution.[45] Jackson himself conceded to James Hamilton that most of the cabinet opposed the president's assertions, a fact he ascribed to "all the sordid and interested who prize self-interest more than the perpetuation of our liberty and blessings of a free republican government."[46] Long-time South Carolina Congressman George McDuffie, then chairing the House Ways and Means committee, attacked Jackson's assertions and issued a report affirming the bank's constitutionality. The report also concluded that the bank had indeed provided a stable national currency. Though McDuffie was an avowed hardmoney man, he nonetheless recognized that this was simply not a practicable monetary system at the current time. According to McDuffie, America faced a simple choice: "a paper currency of uniform value, and subject to the control of the only power competent to its regulation [versus] a paper currency of varying and fluctuating value . . . subject to no common or adequate control whatever."[47]

It is possible that McDuffie's vindication of the bank's policies may have reflected Jackson's growing estrangement from Vice President Calhoun, who was McDuffie's political ally. McDuffie's counterpart in the Senate, Finance Committee Chairman Samuel Smith, also issued a report praising the bank for having established a sound currency and vindicating it of Jackson's attacks. Biddle interpreted McDuffie and Smith's rejection of Jackson's assertions as evidence of strong congressional support for the bank, and he asked his friend William B. Lewis, second auditor of the Treasury, to try to convince the president of the bank's utility. When Lewis met with the president to discuss the bank, Jackson made it clear that he was not looking for a fight with Congress over recharter, but he nevertheless remained opposed to the institution, claiming that it held "exclusive privileges in which the whole people could not share."[48]

Biddle dismissed the president's criticism of the bank, believing it reflected only Jackson's idiosyncratic disdain for banks in general and hoping that it would be frustrated by the cooler heads that surrounded Old Hickory in the cabinet. Writing to Samuel Smith, Biddle confided that Jackson's message "is not therefore a cabinet measure, nor a party measure, but a personal measure. As such it is far less dangerous because if the people know that this is not an opinion which they must necessarily adopt as a portion of their party creed—but an opinion of the President alone—a very honest opinion though a very erroneous one—then the question will be decided on its own merits." Biddle's dismissal of Jackson's rhetoric reflected his own democratic faith; namely, that if properly informed, Americans would see the bank's self-evident value and reject Jackson's demagoguery. Yet the president's attack on the bank still stung, and Biddle complained to a friend that "Constant abuse of the Bank from . . . the official organ of the administration" showed Jackson's determination to "to injure the independence of the Bank."[49]

While in retrospect it is easy to criticize Biddle's failure to take Jackson's attack as seriously as he should have, it is imperative to note that throughout this period, he received contradictory intelligence that made it difficult to understand just how precarious the bank's position really was. In October, Lewis, one of Jackson's closest advisers, wrote to Biddle, claiming, "The President thinks as you do, that the Bank of the U. States should recognize no party; and that, in all its operations, it should have an eye *single* to the interests of the stockholders and the good of the country."[50] According to Kentucky Senator Henry Clay, who was widely expected to run for president in 1832, the bank's real enemy was Secretary of State Van Buren, who sought to use opposition to the bank as a wedge issue to mobilize support for his own political ambitions. In this scenario, the president was not really opposed to the bank—it was all just politics—and, when presented with a recharter bill, he would ultimately sign it for the good of the country, a belief rooted in Biddle's experience that when it really counted, American presidents chose pragmatism over ideology.[51] This, coupled with the president's relative silence on the bank issue during 1830, lulled Biddle into believing that the bank's future was more secure than it was. Jackson's statements during November and December 1829 should leave no doubt as to his intentions regarding the bank, but two other issues—the so-called Petticoat Affair and a showdown with Vice President Calhoun over states' rights—occupied the president's attention for the next two years and gave Biddle a brief respite, perhaps convincing him that the danger had passed. In a letter to a friend, Biddle boasted, "I do not feel the least anxiety about the sortie of the President, who with, I am sure, the best intentions, has erred from want of information."[52] As subsequent events demonstrated, Biddle had misread Old Hickory.

The Petticoat Affair revolved around Secretary of War John Eaton's courting of and marriage to Margaret O'Neale Timberlake. Good looking and wealthy, Eaton was a charming widower who had come to Washington in 1818 following his appointment to the Senate from Tennessee. While in Washington, Eaton roomed at a boardinghouse owned by William O'Neale, and it was there that he met Margaret "Peggy" O'Neale Timberlake. She was married to a navy purser who was frequently out of Washington, and she and Eaton became fast friends, leading some to gossip that the two were having an affair. The gossip only got worse when her husband died while at sea in 1828; some people even claimed he had killed himself after finding out about his wife and Eaton's affair. The couple only added to the gossip by getting married on New Year's Day

1829, a period of mourning that many in Washington saw as indecently short. One joke that was commonly heard had it that "Eaton has just married his mistress, and the mistress of eleven dozen others!"

Due to such unsavory gossip, many of the wives of Jackson's cabinet members refused to associate with Peggy Eaton. Because much of Washington's official business was conducted informally through the process of calling—that is, visiting people's houses—the incoming cabinet members' wives' refusal to socialize with Peggy Eaton was effectively a refusal to socialize with John Eaton, whom Jackson would soon appoint secretary of war.

Worse, the scandal quickly became public. At the inauguration and the ball that followed, the wives of Vice President Calhoun and those of the incoming secretaries of the navy and the Treasury, John Branch and Samuel Ingham, snubbed Peggy Eaton for all to see. In addition, the Petticoat Affair exacerbated divisions within the cabinet. Ever one to personalize a controversy, Jackson saw the gossip about Peggy Eaton as similar to the attacks on Rachel Jackson during the preceding year's presidential election, namely, as unjust aspersions on the honor of a virtuous woman by unscrupulous and scheming politicians. At one point, Jackson exploded during a cabinet meeting, describing Peggy Eaton as "chaste as a virgin!"[53]

Though few would go as far as Jackson in vouching for Peggy Eaton's virtue, Van Buren used the scandal to cement his position in the administration. Calhoun's wife, Floride, led the charge against Peggy Eaton, forcefully asserting that she would not socialize with the Eatons. By contrast, Van Buren, whose wife had died years before, defended the Eatons and continued socializing with them, endearing him to the president. At the end of 1829, Jackson described Van Buren as "everything I could desire him to be . . . frank, open, candid, and manly."[54] By contrast, Calhoun's actions alienated him from Jackson, weakening him and his supporters politically, and the Petticoat Affair paralyzed the new administration, making sustained action against the bank impossible, at least in the short term. Over the long term, however, the net effect was to raise one of the bank's prime enemies (Van Buren) in the president's estimation while simultaneously diminishing the influence of a potential bank ally (Calhoun) with Old Hickory.

The Petticoat Affair revealed another facet of Jackson's personality that directly bore on the Bank War. Historian Donald Cole, who wrote one of the most authoritative histories of Jackson's presidency, argued that Old Hickory came to the White House "a man less sure of himself than imagined."[55] Consequently Jackson, who was ever sensitive to slights (real and imagined), frequently tried to cover his insecurities through bravado and braggadocio. Following a meeting with group of congressmen, during which one implied that Jackson had lost control of the government, Old Hickory railed to his nephew that he would "shew the world" that he was still in charge.[56] Add to that Jackson's penchant for dissimulation and his often violent mood swings and what you have is a recipe for inconsistency that made it impossible for Biddle to accurately predict Jackson's actions.

The Petticoat Affair was not the only political controversy distracting Jackson in spring 1830. On May 27, Jackson vetoed a bill that would have allowed the federal government to purchase stock in the Maysville, Washington, Paris, and Lexington Turnpike Road Company, which had been organized to finance the construction of a road across Kentucky linking Lexington to Maysville. The president's veto represented a sharp break with the past; up until 1830, the federal government frequently helped finance projects like the Maysville Road. Jackson justified his veto by noting:

> The constitutional power of the Federal Government to construct or promote works of internal improvement presents itself in two points of view—the first as bearing upon the sovereignty of the States within whose limits their execution is contemplated, if jurisdiction of the territory which they may occupy be claimed as necessary to their preservation and use; the second as asserting the simple right to appropriate money from the National Treasury in aid of such works when undertaken by State authority, surrendering the claim of jurisdiction. In the first view the question of power is an open one, and can be decided without the embarrassments attending the other, arising from the practice of the Government.

Although frequently and strenuously attempted, the power to this extent has never been exercised by the Government in a single instance. It does not, in my opinion, possess it; and no bill, therefore, which admits it can receive my official sanction.[57]

Jackson's veto alienated those of his supporters who wished the road constructed, and was viewed by more than a few commentators as a petty swipe at former Secretary of State Clay, who had represented Kentucky in the House and the Senate. Others saw in Jackson's veto the hand of Van Buren, who feared that the Maysville Road, if constructed, might imperil Manhattan's rise to economic prominence.

Furthermore, though the Bank War was on the back burner in Spring 1830, and the Maysville Road veto did not explicitly deal with the issue of a national bank, it raised red flags about the president's attitude toward the Bank of the United States. According to Jackson:

The ground taken at an early period of the Government was "that whenever money has been raised by the general authority and is to be applied to a particular measure, a question arises whether the particular measure be within the enumerated authorities vested in Congress. If it be, the money requisite for it may be applied to it; if not, no such application can be made." The document in which this principle was first advanced is of deservedly high authority, and should be held in grateful remembrance for its immediate agency in rescuing the country from much existing abuse and for its conservative effect upon some of the most valuable principles of the Constitution. The symmetry and purity of the Government would doubtless have been better preserved if this restriction of the power of appropriation could have been maintained without weakening its ability to fulfill the general objects of its institution, an effect so likely to attend its admission, notwithstanding its apparent fitness, that every subsequent Administration of the Government, embracing a period of thirty out of the forty-two years of its existence, has adopted a more enlarged construction of the power. . . . This brief reference to known facts will be sufficient to show the difficulty, if not impracticability, of bringing back the operations of the Government to the construction of the Constitution set up in 1798, assuming that to be its true reading in relation to the power under consideration, thus giving an admonitory proof of the force of implication and the necessity of guarding the Constitution with sleepless vigilance against the authority of precedents which have not the sanction of its most plainly defined powers; for although it is the duty of all to look to that sacred instrument instead of the statute book, to repudiate at all times encroachments upon its spirit, which are too apt to be effected by the conjuncture of peculiar and facilitating circumstances, it is not less true that the public good and the nature of our political institutions require that individual differences should yield to a well-settled acquiescence of the people and confederated authorities in particular constructions of the Constitution on doubtful points. Not to concede this much to the spirit of our institutions would impair their stability and defeat the objects of the Constitution itself.[58]

Put another way, Jackson's veto of the Maysville Road bill was rooted in a belief that the federal government had consistently exceeded its constitutional authority in funding internal improvements and that he intended—with "sleepless vigilance"—to fight the erection or continuance of any institution that lacked "the sanction of its most plainly defined powers." Like, for instance, the Bank of the United States.

Another thing distracting Jackson was the brewing fight over nullification, or the doctrine that state governments could refuse to abide by or enforce (nullify) federal laws with which they disagreed. The Tariff of 1828 angered Southerners for two reasons: as a protectionist tariff, it raised the cost of goods for Southern consumers and contributed to lower British imports of Southern cotton. It seemed to Southerners that the tariff's major benefits accrued to the North while the South bore its costs. Ironically, the man largely responsible for the Tariff of 1828 was Martin Van Buren, who saw it as a ploy to improve Jackson's chance of winning that year's presidential election; he had hoped to force President John Quincy Adams to either sign the tariff, thereby enraging Southerners, or veto it and thus alienate his Northern supporters, an excellent illustration of Van Buren's greater willingness to manipulate policy for political advantage. The net effect of the fight over nullification was that it destroyed Jackson's already strained relationship with Calhoun, who might have been a forceful administration voice in support of the bank.

Biddle was also distracted during fall 1831 because of the unexpected death of his younger brother, Thomas, which was indirectly connected with the Bank War. Born in 1790, Thomas Biddle was commissioned as an artillery captain during the early part of the War of 1812. Wounded during the Battle of Lundy's Lane, Thomas Biddle was breveted a major. Following the war, he was transferred to Saint Louis and became a US Army paymaster. In 1823, he married the daughter of a wealthy local businessman and became director of the bank's Saint Louis branch. Thomas Biddle was thus one of the wealthiest and most prominent men in Saint Louis society by 1830 and closely identified with the Bank of the United States. The bank was particularly controversial in Missouri given the leading role that one of its senators, the pugnacious and combative Thomas Hart Benton, played in arousing congressional opposition to its recharter. In 1830, one of Benton's acolytes, Congressman Spencer Pettis, harshly criticized Nicholas Biddle in a speech. Thomas Biddle responded to Pettis's comments, and a war of words quickly erupted between the two proud men, especially after Pettis disparaged Thomas Biddle's manhood. Things turned violent in July 1831 when Thomas Biddle attacked an ill Pettis in the latter's hotel room, severely beating the sick man with a cowhide whip.

Fearing a further attack, Pettis petitioned the local court for a peace warrant to arrest Biddle. When Biddle appeared at the hearing to defend himself, Pettis tried to shoot Biddle with a pistol but was restrained by friends. Seeing this, Biddle dared Pettis to call him out for a duel, and the congressman later obliged. Under the *code duello*, or the rules of dueling, Thomas Biddle (as the man challenged to the duel) had the right to select the weapons and the starting distance. Being nearsighted, Biddle chose pistols and announced that the men would only be five feet away from one another, leading some to speculate that Biddle was trying to intimidate Pettis into backing down. If this was the case, Biddle's plan failed miserably, and the two men met on the aptly named Bloody Island, a small sandbar in the Mississippi River near Saint Louis. As prescribed, they fired at one another from a distance of five feet, and each inflicted mortal wounds on the other. According to legend, as the men were taken from Bloody Island, each forgave the other. In any event, Pettis died the next day while Biddle survived for two excruciating days before finally succumbing to his wounds on August 29. The Biddle-Pettis duel, though an extreme case, demonstrates how bitter and divisive the conflict over the bank's future had become, and it presaged the rancorous political showdown over the bank's recharter.

Meanwhile, Jackson continued his Janus-faced approach to dealing with the bank's supporters.

On May 25, William Lewis wrote to Biddle claiming that, "In conversing with [Jackson] a few days ago upon [the bank] he still entertained the opinion that a *National* Bank might be established that would be preferable to the president than the U.S. Bank; but that, if Congress thought differently, and it was deemed necessary to such a Bank as the present, with certain modifications he should not object to it."[59] In midsummer, Nashville branch president John Nichol reported to Biddle a conversation he had with Jackson about the bank. Jackson banked at the Nashville branch, and Nichol considered the president a personal friend. Nichol wrote to Biddle, claiming that Jackson "appears to be well satisfied with the facilities that the Bank have given to the government and the individuals in transferring the funds from one point to another and acknowledges that a Bank such as the present only can do so. He appears to be generally pleased with the management of the Bank of the United States and branches—and particularly so with this office." Though Nichols informed Biddle that Jackson was in the habit of keeping his thoughts to himself, the Nashville branch's president belied this assertion by informing Biddle that the president's only real concern was that foreigners owned a majority of the bank's stock.[60]

If Nichols' words soothed Biddle's worries, a letter he received a few weeks later from former Treasury Secretary Albert Gallatin should have aroused his concern. Gallatin told Biddle that in New York, there was considerable opposition to the bank, whose main proponent, Van Buren, had the president's ear. Gallatin warned Biddle that Jackson could not be trusted, having "prematurely and gratuitously declared himself [on the bank issue] and given the signal of attack to his adherents."61 This message reinforced a letter that Biddle had received from Henry Clay in which the House speaker claimed "the plan was laid at Richmond during a visit made to that place by the Secy. Of State last autumn, to make the destruction of the bank the basis of the Presidential Election. The message of the President, and other indications, are the supposed consequences of that plan."62

In December 1830, Jackson issued his second annual message, which criticized the bank harshly and sketched an alternate plan that the president claimed would address the constitutional issues. According to Jackson:

> The importance of the principles involved in the inquiry whether it will be proper to recharter the Bank of the United States requires that I should again call the attention of Congress to the subject. Nothing has occurred to lessen in any degree the dangers which many of our citizens apprehend from that institution as at present organized. In the spirit of improvement and compromise which distinguishes our country and its institutions it becomes us to inquire whether it be not possible to secure the advantages afforded by the present bank through the agency of a Bank of the United States so modified in its principles and structures as to obviate constitutional and other objections.
>
> It is thought practicable to organize such a bank with the necessary officers as a branch of the Treasury Department, based on the public and individual deposits, without power to make loans or purchase property, which shall remit the funds of the Government, and the expense of which may be paid, if thought advisable, by allowing its officers to sell bills of exchange to private individuals at a moderate premium. Not being a corporate body, having no stock

holders, debtors, or property, and but few officers, it would not be obnoxious to the constitutional objections which are urged against the present bank; and having no means to operate on the hopes, fears, or interests of large masses of the community, it would be shorn of the influence which makes that bank formidable. The States would be strengthened by having in their hands the means of furnishing the local paper currency through their own banks, while the Bank of the United States, though issuing no paper, would check the issues of the State banks by taking their notes in deposit and for exchange only so long as they continue to be redeemed with specie. In times of public emergency the capacities of such an institution might be enlarged by legislative provisions.

Interestingly, despite Jackson's obvious hostility toward the bank and his clearly expressed belief that it was unconstitutional, he again hedged his statements, claiming, "These suggestions are made not so much as a recommendation as with a view of calling the attention of Congress to the possible modifications of a system which can not continue to exist in its present form without occasional collisions with the local authorities and perpetual apprehensions and discontent on the part of the States and the people."[63]

But Biddle was still receiving contradictory intelligence, mostly because Jackson intentionally misled their mutual acquaintances. Less than two weeks after the president issued his second annual message, Robert Smith wrote to Biddle, recounting a conversation William Lewis had with Jackson. Lewis claimed to Smith that the president would recharter the bank provided that Biddle accepted some minor face-saving changes to its structure and powers. Smith elaborated on this claim, telling Biddle, "I gathered from a conversation with Major Lewis, of the Presidents family, that altho' the President is decidedly in favor of a Bank such as he recommended to Congress, yet if a bill were to pass both houses, renewing the charter of the Bank of the U. States, with certain modifications, the President would not withhold his approval."[64] There can be little doubt that Lewis got this impression because Jackson gave it to him. Manipulation and deceit were just two of Jackson's political weapons, and this incident was an excellent illustration of his capacity for dissimulation.

After two years of essentially allowing the president to abuse the bank in public while the administration sent mixed signals about its intentions, in early 1831, Biddle concluded that he had to answer Jackson's charges or lose the battle for public opinion. Believing that if armed with "truth and reason," American voters would support rechartering the bank, Biddle used bank funds to purchase space in newspapers to rebut Jackson's claims. His goal was to combat the opposition's "downright ignorance . . . through the free circulation of honest truths by means of the press."[65]

In so doing, however, he played directly into the president's hands by seemingly using the bank's vast wealth for political purposes. This, coupled with the fact that the bank loaned money to the editors of a New York newspaper explicitly to gain favorable editorials, backfired on Biddle when the administration's supporters began citing these expenditures as proof of the president's assertions regarding the bank's corrupting influence, a point that Roger Taney made in 1849 when he asserted that the bank's "most dangerous . . . and formidable power when it entered the political arena was the corrupt and corrupting influence it . . . had acquired over the press. In every state where a Branch was established some one or more of the leading news papers were devoted to its interests. Even without any direct bribery, every paper would naturally desire the favor of the institution on account [of] the facilities it could afford [the paper's owner] in his business."[66] The fact that the Jackson administration had its own newspaper in the *Globe* that survived largely on federal printing contracts seems not to have troubled Taney.

That spring, another event occurred that, though not directly related to Jackson's brewing conflict with the bank, was to have long-term effects on the administration's policy. The Petticoat Affair had seriously hampered the administration, and two years into Jackson's term, the scandal still vexed the president. By early 1831, Van Buren recognized that a change in the cabinet was required to put the scandal to rest, but he also knew that Jackson could not ask for the offending cabinet members' resignations without tacitly admitting that he was doing so in response their wives' refusal to socialize with Peggy Eaton. In late March, Van Buren resigned as secretary of state, and he was soon followed by Secretary of War Eaton, which gave Jackson a pretext for pressuring the other members of his cabinet to resign. Ingham, Navy Secretary Branch, and Attorney General John M. Berrien all did so, though only after making public that they were leaving under pressure. This only added to the controversy, with Jackson's political opponents pointing out that the breakup of the cabinet was unprecedented in the history of the republic. Moreover, Jackson was embarrassed by the fact that the sole remaining member of his cabinet, Postmaster General William T. Berry, was generally regarded as incompetent and was being investigated by the Senate. A widely circulated political cartoon captured Jackson's opponents' delight at the president's troubles, depicting Old Hickory in a collapsing chair while the various cabinet members are depicted as rats fleeing the administration.

Jackson immediately moved to rebuild his cabinet, though this time he chose members more carefully with an eye toward upcoming battles with Congress. He appointed Louisiana Senator Edward Livingston secretary of state and the long-time territorial governor of Michigan, Lewis Cass, secretary of war. Former attorney general of Maryland Roger Taney became US attorney general, while former New Hampshire Governor Levi Woodbury became secretary of the navy. Perhaps most important, from Biddle's perspective, was Jackson's selection of former Delaware Senator Louis McLane as secretary of the Treasury. Jackson's choices reflected the diverse nature of the Jacksonian coalition but were united in two key respects: one was their shared hostility to Calhoun and the other was the fact that many of the new men appeared to be supporters of the bank. Unfortunately for the president, this was not a recipe for a harmonious or united cabinet; as the next chapter makes clear, Jackson was forced by political necessity to appoint to key posts men not wholly sympathetic to his war on the bank, and the new cabinet would be as riven by factionalism as the old one. Consequently, as historian Donald Cole noted, while the new cabinet met frequently, "the old General never became comfortable with his cabinet," and

"Rats Leaving a Falling House." An anti-administration political cartoon depicting the resignations of Jackson's cabinet members. The anonymous cartoonist is arguing that the administration is collapsing and the elderly Jackson in unable to prevent it. (*Library of Congress*)

the various members were frequently at cross-purposes, both with one another and with the president.[67]

Meanwhile, Jackson appointed Van Buren minister to Great Britain. This represented a step back for the former secretary of state; though he had won the fight with Calhoun for Jackson's affection, it was nonetheless true that the Petticoat Affair had weakened the New Yorker as well. Van Buren would, at least temporarily, be denied the easy access to the president that he enjoyed as secretary of state. One contemporary gleefully noted that Van Buren would be "out of sight, out of mind," while many of the New Yorker's friends described him as sullen and morose in the lead up to his departure from Washington.[68]

For his part, Biddle was pleased at the composition of Jackson's new cabinet, believing that the new appointees—particularly Secretary of State Livingston and Secretary of the Treasury McLane—supported the bank. He also saw Van Buren's exile to Great Britain as a stroke of good luck, believing that the New Yorker was primarily responsible for the president's prejudices toward the bank. On May 4, Biddle crowed, "In regard to politics and politicians, the explosion [of the president's cabinet] . . . has given a new aspect to the state of things. I consider it a fortunate change for the bank by the substitution of an avowed friend, Mr. [Edward] Livingston [as Secretary of State], for a decided enemy in Mr. Van Buren. The new Secretary of the Treasury [Louis McLane] is also a known friend and generally speaking the occurrence I consider fortunate." In fact, Jackson's new cabinet almost unanimously supported rechartering the Bank of the United States, so at first glance events seemed to have justified Biddle's optimism. Believing that the cabinet would restrain the president, Biddle reiterated his belief that the bank (and those associated with it) should stay out of politics, writing, "I should lament deeply that those connected with the bank should be active or zealous or conspicuous in political contests. This would be wrong in itself, it is a violation of that perfect neutrality which is the first duty of the Bank. It would be injudicious too, even on calculation, since no advantage to be derived from their efforts would overbalance the general evil from their actual or supposed influence."[69]

Events over the next few months seemed to justify Biddle's optimism. Most of Jackson's third annual message dealt with foreign affairs; he did not mention the Bank of the United States until the very end of the message and then only briefly. According to Jackson:

> Entertaining the opinions heretofore expressed in relation to the Bank of the United States as at present organized, I felt it my duty in my former messages frankly to disclose them, in order that the attention of the Legislature and the people should be seasonably directed to that important subject, and that it might be considered and finally disposed of in a manner best calculated to promote the ends of the Constitution and subserve the public interests. Having thus conscientiously discharged a constitutional duty, I deem it proper on this occasion, without a more particular reference to the views of the subject then expressed to leave it for the present to the investigation of an enlightened people and their representatives.[70]

This was far more temperate language than he had used the year before, leading some observers to conclude that Jackson's new cabinet had managed to soften Old Hickory's animus toward the bank. Jackson again called on Congress to address the constitutional issues allegedly raised by the bank's charter, though he refrained from attacking the institution directly.

A few weeks after Jackson transmitted his message to Congress, Treasury Secretary McLane sent his own message, which endorsed rechartering the bank. Years later, Van Buren criticized McLane for having "thrown his official shield around the Bank in his first annual report upon the finances." Interestingly, Van Buren also quoted a letter that McLane sent him which offers a glimpse of how the fight over rechartering the bank was rapidly turning into a test of Democratic Party bona fides. According to Van Buren, before forwarding his annual report to Congress, McLane sent the New Yorker a copy of it along with a note that said, "You will not approve of this report most probably—unless you purge your mind, not of your democracy, but of your party prejudices. If you take up the spirit of the patriot, you will bless me for [the report]."[71]

It is striking that in his note to Van Buren, McLane drew a distinction between democratic principles and party prejudices, suggesting that these were not necessarily the same thing. In fact, McLane seems to be arguing that men truly committed to democratic principles—as oppose to Democrats—should celebrate the recharter of the bank, implying that the Jacksonian war against the bank in some sense represented a rejection of democratic values. Regardless of the validity of McLane's argument, the fact that he made it shows that while opposition to the bank was quickly becoming the acid test of Democratic Party loyalty, some holdouts remained uncommitted to destroying the bank.

However, this debate was largely happening behind the scenes. Certainly, someone reading Jackson and McLane's messages to Congress could reasonably have concluded that the president's aversion to the bank had cooled, or that at the very least, Jackson had decided to live with the bank for the time being. Even Taney conceded that the president was sending mixed signals, calling Jackson's message "ambiguous and indecisive."[72] In retrospect, Taney noted:

> [T]he truth was that the ambiguous tone of the [president's] message followed by the report of the Secretary of the Treasury [in favor of the Bank] had perplexed and mystified the friends of Genl. Jackson and weakened the opposition to the <renewal of the charter which up to that time had been daily gaining in strength>. His political opponents regarded these measures as proof that he feared the influence of the bank and its friends in the approaching election of President, and was either retreating from his old ground, or seeking to evade the issue until the election was over.[73]

This was certainly the message Biddle was receiving; after all, Congressman Samuel Smith claimed in a letter to the bank president that the annual message "shows that [Jackson is wavering]. If pressed into a *corner* immediately, neither McLane nor myself will answer for the consequences. But we both feel confident of the ultimate success if time be given for the president to convince himself of the error into which opinion long formed (prejudice if you please) has committed him."[74]

What Biddle missed was the fact that Jackson's main advisers now operated behind the scenes, and they were not at all friendly to the bank. Though Jackson met frequently with the new cabinet, he had identified a small coterie of outside advisers—Amos Kendall, Senator Benton, and Congressman James K. Polk—on whom he relied for political advice. This informal group of advisers became known to opponents as the Kitchen Cabinet, reflecting the belief that it met informally in the White House kitchen instead of in the mansion's parlor. The members of this group were far more ideological than the members of the cabinet, and to a man they were committed to the bank's extirpation. As a result, the cabinet's probank

Louis McLane. (*Library of Congress*)

tendencies did not actually influence policy. When it became clear later that Jackson's main advisers were not his official cabinet members, Biddle expressed his fears, saying, "What I have dreaded about this new cabinet was that the kitchen would predominate over the parlor."[75]

Biddle was right to be concerned; the Kitchen Cabinet was far more hostile to the bank than the official cabinet. In his autobiography, former Kitchen Cabinet member and Postmaster General Kendall described the Bank of the United States' formation this way:

> When the government was organized under the Constitution, a Treasurer was appointed to receive the public money, carefully keep it, and to pay it out only "in consequence of appropriations made by law." . . . But there was a class of men who desired to obtain the public money for private uses. They did not like this system, which kept the money in the Treasury for the public only; and they set themselves at work to overthrow it. An ingenious plan was hit upon to abolish the Treasury, make the Treasurer a bookkeeper only, and take the money that should be in the Treasury for the use of merchant, speculators, and other borrowers. The plan was to hand over the public money to banks, not to be *kept*, but to be *lent*. . . . Bank stockholders pocketed the interest, and the

Constitution became in this respect a dead letter. To perfect the scheme, a Bank of the United States was created, being the most convenient instrument through which the public money could be applied to private purposes.[76]

The net effect was that Jackson was now surrounded by people far more uniformly hostile to the bank, which only reinforced Jackson's determination to curtail its power and influence.

That being said, Jackson was also committed to keeping the bank issue out of the upcoming presidential campaign. In October, Biddle met with McLane, who told him, "the Pres. is perfectly confident of his election—the only question is the greater or the less majority, but he is sure of success & wishes to succeed by a greater vote than at the first election." The implication was clear: Jackson's reelection took precedence over his concerns about the bank, at least temporarily, and the president was loath to do anything that might cost him votes. Yet McLane also passed along a not-so-subtle threat: should Biddle try to corner the president into rechartering the bank during the presidential election, Jackson "might on that account be disposed to put his veto on it."[77] McLane's statement to Biddle certainly explains the more temperate tone in the president's third annual message. Not wanting to alienate Biddle, who might force the divisive recharter issue, Jackson softened his rhetoric. In a memo to himself about Jackson's impending third annual message, Biddle wrote, "The President is to say that having previously brought the [issue of rechartering the bank] to Congress, he now leaves it with them. The Secretary [of the Treasury] is to recommend the renewal. This later point pleases me much."[78]

While this might at first glance appear to be a victory for the bank, it is important not to read too much into McLane's statement. At no point did Jackson promise to sign a recharter bill after the election; he merely threatened—through the Treasury secretary—to veto any such bill that crossed his desk before the presidential election. It was the classic heads-I-win-tails-you-lose proposition: Jackson would get what he wanted (no divisive political issues to depress his vote total in key states like Pennsylvania) while retaining his freedom of action when it came to the bank, which had to be rechartered no later than March 1836. In fact, in a letter to John Randolph, a former Virginia senator and minister to Russia, Jackson actually repudiated McLane's statements to Biddle. Jackson wrote:

> Mr. McLane has on his own authority, in conformity with his sense of a positive duty which he did not feel at liberty to disregard and which it would have been unbecoming in me to control ventured the expression that [the bank] might be so modified as to strip it of the constitutional objections entertained by the executive. In saying this it was far from his intention or wish to be understood as committing me, in any manner to the friends of the bank in support of any schedule for obtaining a new charter.[79]

Furthermore, while he had tempered his rhetoric and allowed McLane to recommend renewing the bank's charter, Jackson had a long history of telling people one thing and doing another, which Biddle had experienced firsthand. In sum, there was no reason for Biddle to believe that once Jackson was reelected and no longer cared about raising a divisive issue like the bank, he would acquiesce to its recharter. That being said, moving ahead with the recharter petition was guaranteed to provoke Jackson and lead to a showdown with the president. Assuming that the recharter bill passed both houses of Congress, Jackson would almost surely veto it. Reporting to Biddle on a conversation he had with Pennsylvania Senator George M. Dallas, Thomas Cadwalader noted that while Dallas was disposed to helping the bank any way he could, "he hangs in doubt as to the policy of starting the application *now*, unless it can be ascertained that we have 2/3d [necessary to override a presidential veto]."[80] In other words, if Biddle planned on picking a fight with Jackson over the bank's charter, he had better make sure he had the votes to win.

It was at this juncture that Henry Clay, who had just returned to Congress as a senator from Kentucky, reached out to Biddle. Clay was planning to challenge Jackson for the presidency in 1832, and a divisive political issue that would split the president's supporters was exactly what Clay wanted to see on the national agenda. He was joined in this regard by a number of prominent anti-Jacksonians, including Senator Daniel Webster of Massachusetts, and Biddle's personal friend John Sergeant (who joined Clay on the Whig ticket in 1832).[81] Two years earlier, Clay had counseled Biddle to act cautiously, arguing that precipitously pushing for early recharter of the bank would play into Van Buren's hands by giving the New Yorker an issue on which to run for president in 1832.[82] Apparently, the Kentuckian had changed his mind; a little more than a week after Jackson's third annual message, Clay stocked Biddle's fears about Jackson's attitude toward the bank. Clay wrote:

> Have you come to any decision about an application to Congress at this Session for the renewal of your Charter? The friends of the bank here, with whom I have conversed, seem to expect the application to be made. The course of the President in the event of the passage of a bill, seems to be a matter of doubt and speculation. My own belief is that, if now called upon he would not negative the bill, but that if he should be re-elected the event might and probably would be different.[83]

This was hardly friendly or disinterested advice; Clay was less concerned about the bank's future than he was about hurting the president politically and thereby improving his own chances in the election. Clearly, Jackson's antipathy toward the bank had turned the debate over its recharter into a partisan football, and for that very reason Clay salivated at the prospect of forcing the president to make a politically costly decision: veto the recharter or sign it. That being said, however, Clay's analysis was sound: the looming election gave Biddle the maximum amount of leverage he would ever have over Jackson, and the president had already proven himself duplicitous and dishonest in his dealings with the bank president. In short, pushing for recharter before the presidential election was Biddle's best chance to win the Bank War.

Intrigued by the idea, Biddle sent Cadwalader to Washington to ascertain how much support existed in Congress for rechartering the bank. Cadwalader spoke with various members of Congress and with Treasury Secretary McLane and reported to Biddle that small majorities in both houses likely supported rechartering the bank.

Though McLane advised Cadwalader against pushing for recharter in 1832, the latter argued that Biddle should move ahead, and on January 6, Biddle made the fateful step of formally notifying House Ways and Means Committee Chair George McDuffie and Senate Finance Committee Chair Samuel Smith that he would soon submit a petition requesting that Congress consider the bank's application for recharter.[84] This was a monumental shift in Biddle's strategy: henceforth, the bank would no longer try to appease the administration. Jackson's dissimulation over the past three years convinced Biddle he had to take his chances with Congress, and the only leverage he had over the president was the looming election.

Biddle's request for recharter opened a new, more hostile phase in the Bank War. Three days later, Biddle submitted the petition to Senator Dallas. That same day, Biddle was unanimously reelected to the bank's presidency, an event the banker saw as a mandate for pressing the recharter bill. In a letter, North Carolina Senator Willie P. Mangum, one of the bank's friends in Congress, asserted, "I have no doubt with but slight modification (to save appearances) [the bank's charter] would have met with Executive favor.—It is *now* more than doubtful whether it will.—And the whole may ultimately take the appearance of a trile of strength between Gen Jackson & the Bank.—In all case the Bank will go down—for Gen J's popularity is of *a sort* not to slaken [sic] at present."[85]

Predictably, Jackson was furious, seeing Biddle's actions as a personal slight and a signal that he had lost control of the government. Taney, Jackson's attorney general, perfectly captured the administration's confrontational attitude about the recharter when he noted in a letter, "I understand the application at the present time, it means in plain English this—the Bank says to the President, your next election is at hand—if you charter us, well—if not, beware your power."[86] The president took zero responsibility for the ambiguous and contradictory signals he and his administration had broadcast regarding the bank over the past three years, and he refused to admit that he was, in fact, playing a double game with Biddle over the bank's recharter. Raging at James Hamilton, Jackson exploded, "I will prove to them that I never flinch, that they were mistaken when they expect to act upon me by such considerations."[87] Jackson's proclamation aside, the fight over the bank's recharter solidified the process under way by which the bank question had become the primary test of loyalty to the Democratic Party. Henceforth, the president actively worked to make opposition to the bank Democratic Party orthodoxy, a course that over the next year forced Jackson to purge his cabinet of men insufficiently committed to the bank's destruction. The bare-knuckle tactics he employed against the bank helped coalesce his opponents into an organized political party. In sum, the debate over the bank's future had become a war, and Jackson had no intention of losing.

4

The President versus
the Banker

In his memoirs, Martin Van Buren recalled one of the Bank War's most dramatic and telling moments. Having recently returned to the United States from Great Britain, where he had served briefly as Jackson's ambassador to the Court of St. James's, Van Buren made his way to the White House one summer evening. There he found an ailing president "stretched on a sick-bed a spectre in physical appearance but as always a hero in spirit." Grasping Van Buren's hand, Jackson said to him "with the clearest indications of a mind composed, and in a tone entirely devoid of passion or bluster—'the bank, Mr. Van Buren is trying to kill me, *but I will kill it!*'"[1] While it is hard to imagine Jackson delivering these stirring words in "a tone entirely devoid of passion or bluster," better than anything else, Jackson's statement encapsulates the essential feature of the second phase of the Bank War, namely, it was personal, aggressive, and a fight to the death. Through his unbridled hostility to the bank and his disingenuousness over the course of his first term, Jackson had created the very monster he always feared. Now, in the lead-up to reelection, he would slay the monster or die trying.

Raising the issue of recharter in 1832 and Jackson's subsequent veto of the recharter bill politicized what should have been an economic issue. Jackson's hatred of the bank also became party orthodoxy: now, Democrats had to "be right" on the bank. In fact, Jackson's economic policies, and the political battles they spawned, were the crucible that formed the Democratic Party. As historian Frank Otto Gatell notes, this was the moment when Democrats who had been favorably disposed to the bank had to make a choice: Jackson and the rapidly coalescing party or Biddle and the still-disorganized and fragmented opposition. According to Gatell, "Jackson had cracked the whip, and most Jacksonians responded."[2] Though the Democrats still had factions, the heat generated by the Bank War nonetheless forged them into a more unified and coherent political party that would win four of the seven presidential elections from 1836 to 1860. It also helped crystallize the opposition into a political party—the Whigs—and thereby gave birth to the Second Party System.

Once Biddle took the fateful step of applying for recharter, Jackson took every opportunity available to him to attack the bank and its interests. At nearly the same moment as the recharter fight, another conflict between Jackson and the bank appeared. Jackson was committed to continuing and, if possible, accelerating the repayment of the national debt that began in the 1810s. Now Jackson saw an opportunity to achieve two goals—pay down the debt and wound the bank—in one fell swoop. In March 1832, the administration notified the bank that it intended to repay about $6.5 million in bonds on July 1. Unfortunately, the bank was short on funds at that particular moment, and Biddle pleaded with the administration to postpone the payment. The White House refused Biddle's pleas and made it known that it intended to pay another $6.5 million in bonds on January 1. In other words, the bank would have to produce $13 million in less than a year. A payment of that scale would require

Biddle to call in the bank's loans, a move that would starve the economy of liquidity and might even touch off a recession.

In order to avoid draining that much money from the economy and thereby possibly causing a recession, Biddle developed an ingenious scheme: He appealed to the bondholders to turn in the bonds, which would in turn be given to the Treasury Department as evidence that the debt had been paid. In exchange, the Bank of the United States (as opposed to the United States of America) would borrow an equal amount of money from the bondholders in question and continue making interest payments. This was not a violation of the bank's charter, though it certainly contravened the spirit of Jackson's policy of paying down the debt and frustrated the president's goal of weakening the bank. Worse, from Old Hickory's perspective, the execution—which involved the bank's outright buying the bonds at a discount (as opposed to securing a loan from the bondholders in the form of the bonds themselves)—*was* a violation of its charter that, when it became public, did nothing to endear Biddle to Jackson. In fact, when the president became aware of Biddle's clever sleight of hand, he railed to his cabinet that his policies had been thwarted. Jackson complained that Biddle had actively frustrated the administration's policies by "preventing the creditors from doing what they had been called upon by the Government to do. And here the Bank is presented as a Treasury agent defeating the most cherished policy of the Government." Biddle's actions only reinforced Jackson's fears about the bank's power; he asserted that the bank had brought "the great Bankers of Europe as its allies in controlling the affairs of the Republic" and predicted "a new era may possibly arise in the progress of a few years in which the capitalist abroad may have an influence over the destinies of this country akin to that exercised by them in States beyond the Atlantic."

By contrast, Biddle could not understand Jackson's irritation. In a letter to a friend, he observed, "Supposing that the [bonds] are delayed a few months . . . what harm does that do to anybody? The interest has stopped—the money remains in the Treasury; so that instead of depriving the Government of the use of its funds, directly the reverse is true, for the Government retains the funds and pays no interest."[3] Biddle simply could not conceive that Jackson would be willing to damage America's economy just to wound the bank; his surprise was a mark of how little he understood his opponent.

This incident, which is a relatively minor skirmish in the overall Bank War, nonetheless tells us a great deal about Biddle's and Jackson's perspectives and helps explain why a seemingly unexciting topic like central banking became such an explosive political issue. For Biddle, the most important goal was good policy, which he saw as independent of patronage concerns and nonpartisan. He believed that only the bank was capable of formulating this policy and that what was good for the bank was good for the United States. From his perspective, he had achieved Jackson's ends—the United States Treasury was no longer responsible for the interest payments on this portion of the national debt—in the most responsible and least painful way possible. Jackson, by contrast, saw himself—the only federal government official elected by the whole country—as the embodiment of the public will. In his mind, frustrating the administration's wishes was tantamount to violating the public's will, and the fact that Biddle had essentially manipulated the structure of the debt without actually paying it off only reinforced Jackson's fears about the paper money and the banking sector. In other words, what was for Biddle a virtue was for Jackson a vice, and vice versa.

Jackson selected Benton to lead the fight in the Senate against the bank's recharter. Thomas Hart Benton earned his nickname—"Old Bullion"—through his unflagging advocacy of hard money, and he was that faction's informal leader in the Senate. Benton was born in North Carolina in 1782 to a wealthy plantation owner and lawyer. Expelled from the University of North Carolina for theft, Benton eventually moved to Nashville, where he attracted Jackson's attention. Jackson made the thirty-year-old Benton his aide-de-camp during the War of 1812, and he was sent to Washington to represent his commander's interests in the capital. Jackson and Benton's relationship eventually soured, and in 1813, the two men found themselves on opposite sides of a frontier brawl that ended with Benton shooting Jackson, who carried the bullet in his arm until 1832. Following the war, Benton moved to Saint Louis, where he practiced law. Following the Missouri Compromise of 1820 (which made Missouri a state), Benton was elected to the US Senate.

Following the presidential election of 1824, Benton mended fences with Jackson and the two became stalwart political allies. Once Jackson became president in 1829, Benton became the Democrats' de facto leader in the Senate, working to advance his two great passions: westward expansion and hard money. A skilled orator and a fierce oppo-

Thomas Hart Benton. (*Library of Congress*)

nent of the bank, Benton was the ideal point man in the Senate, and he had been champing at the bit to pick a fight with the bank for at least a year. In February 1831, Benton had introduced a resolution to the Senate that the bank should not be rechartered and then launched into a vitriolic attack on the bank.[4] When senators favorable to the bank failed to respond to Benton's speech, which was printed and widely distributed around the country, Biddle published his own attack, claiming that Benton's tirade was "founded upon a want of knowledge of fact, or a total misapprehension of fact."[5]

As he was wont to do, Biddle misinterpreted the contest, seeing it as a debate over policy when in fact it was really a political knife fight to the death, a point that Benton drove home when the then-long-time senator called the 1831–1832 congressional session "one of the most excitedly partisan and one of the most fatiguing in the history of the Congress up to the mid-century." Comparing it to a siege, Benton said the fight over the bank was "fierce in the beginning and becoming more so from day to day until the last hour of the last day of the exhausted session."[6]

Biddle appears to have seen the bank recharter bill as one-half of a carrot–and–stick approach to dealing with the president. Having raised a divisive issue that would damage Jackson's reelection campaign, Biddle now extended a fig leaf. On February 6, Biddle asked Senator Dallas to meet with the president in order to give Jackson a resolution passed by the Pennsylvania legislature imploring the president not to anger voters in the state by vetoing the bank's recharter. Dallas passed the resolution along to the president, but he also made Jackson aware of the fact that Biddle was willing to work with the administration to craft a recharter bill that both sides could live with, thereby obviating the need for a protracted fight in Congress. Three days later, Pennsylvania Congressman Charles J. Ingersoll, met with Secretary of State Edward Livingston and discussed a compromise bill based on Jackson's objections to the bank. Specifically, the federal government would divest itself of bank stock, though the president would retain the right to appoint directors and some branch officials. In addition, states could tax bank branches operating within their borders, a repudiation of the *McCulloch* decision. Almost immediately, Biddle agreed to these terms. In a letter to Ingersoll, he declared: "To me all other considerations [beyond the bank's recharter] are insignificant—I mean to stand by [the bank] & defend it with all the small faculties which Providence has assigned to me. I care for no party in politics or religion—have no sympathy with Mr. Jackson or Mr. Clay. . . . I am for the Bank & the Bank alone."[7]

Even at this late hour, Biddle remained steadfast in his nonpartisan attachment to the bank and refused to make the struggle over recharter personal. He did not actually want to see the bank politicized, which distinguished him from almost all of his congressional allies, who very much wanted to make the fight over the bank as personal and partisan as possible.

While it looked as though a final showdown between Jackson and Biddle had been averted, Benton did everything in his power to scotch the compromise, seeing the fight over the bank as the ideal time to advance his hard-money agenda. A few weeks after Ingersoll and Livingston sketched out a compromise bill, Benton got freshman Representative Augustine S. Clayton of Georgia to introduce a House resolution calling for the bank to be investigated. Benton's goal was to delay as long as possible a vote on the Ingersoll-

Livingston compromise bill in order to shift public opinion against the bank. Clayton's resolution was an ideal trap: if the bank's supporters assented to it, the investigation would delay a vote on the recharter bill, but if they opposed the bill, Benton could plausibly argue that the bank's administration had something to hide. Thus, Clayton's resolution passed the House on March 14, and the administration immediately suspended all negotiations with the bank pending the investigation's outcome.[8]

Clayton's investigation dragged on for six weeks and was a thoroughly partisan affair that resulted in three reports: a majority report heavily critical of the bank, a minority report that dissented from the majority's conclusions, and a report by former President John Quincy Adams, now a congressman from Massachusetts. The majority's report attacked the bank as unconstitutional and a threat to the country's economy, while the two minority reports criticized the majority's ignorance of banking. Clayton's investigation succeeded in its goals: it delayed a vote on the compromise recharter bill and it sowed confusion about the bank. Recognizing that Clayton's investigation had potentially derailed the Ingersoll-Livingston compromise, Biddle traveled to the capital in May to try to salvage the deal. He met with Secretary of State Livingston and Treasury Secretary McLane, both of whom confided that there was little they could do; the majority report from Clayton's committee only reinforced Jackson's conviction that the bank was thoroughly corrupt, and the president was more committed than ever to preventing its recharter. More disconcertingly, a number of probank congressmen pleaded with Biddle to withdraw the recharter bill. They argued that the president would surely veto it, placing them in the awkward position of having either to sustain Jackson's veto or vote to override it and thereby earn the president's lasting enmity. Sympathetic though he may have been to their position, Biddle refused to withdraw the bill, figuring that the impending presidential election gave him the best possible chance of securing renewal.

Thus, on May 23, the bill came before the Senate, which passed it 28 to 20. The recharter bill imposed a number of restrictions on the bank that were designed to address some of the milder criticisms and thereby make the bank more palatable to wavering Democratic congressmen. For instance, while it authorized Biddle to hire at least two officers whose sole responsibility would be to sign bank notes of less than $100 (thereby relieving Biddle of this time-consuming and tedious task), it prohibited the bank from issuing branch bank drafts, holding real estate for more than five years, and opening more than two branches in any state (those currently in operation were excluded). Moreover, the bill required the bank to pay the United States $200,000 annually and gave Congress the right to prohibit it from issuing bank notes in denominations below twenty dollars. All of these changes were designed to assuage the constitutional concerns that Jackson had raised and to get the state banks' support for recharter.[9] Three weeks after the Senate vote, the House followed suit, passing the recharter bill 107 to 85. When one congressman mentioned to Clay that the president would almost certainly veto the bill, Clay defiantly boasted, "should Jackson veto it, I shall veto him!"[10] All of these concessions were for naught; Jackson vetoed the recharter bill.

Jackson was no stranger to vetoing legislation; during his two terms, he not only issued more vetoes than any of his predecessors individually, he issued more vetoes than all previous presidents combined, a fact that led Clay to claim the president's actions "borrowed from the prerogative of the British king."[11] In the recharter bill's case, Jackson issued a pocket veto, which meant that rather than officially veto the legislation, Jackson simply refused to sign the bill and return it to Congress within the ten-day period mandated by the Constitution.

On July 10, Jackson issued a carefully worded statement justifying his refusal to sign the bill. According to Jackson's veto message, while, "A bank of the United States is in many respects convenient for the Government and useful to the people," the president had nonetheless concluded that "some of the powers and privileges possessed by the existing bank are unauthorized by the Constitution, subversive of the rights of the States, and dangerous to the liberties of the people."[12] Claiming that, "in the act before me I can perceive none of those modifications of the bank charter which are necessary, in my opinion, to make it compatible with justice, with sound policy, or with the Constitution of our country," Jackson went on to argue that the bank's charter conferred on its stockholders a monopoly that would transfer to them Americans' wealth. Furthermore, he asserted, "if we must have a bank with private stockholders, every consideration of sound policy and every impulse of American feeling admonishes that it should be *purely American.* Its stockholders should be composed exclusively of our own citizens, who at least ought to be friendly to our Government and willing to support it in times of difficulty and danger."

Jackson also took aim squarely at the precedent established in *McCulloch v. Maryland*, claiming:

> Upon the formation of the Constitution the States guarded their taxing power with peculiar jealousy. They surrendered it only as it regards imports and exports. In relation to every other object within their jurisdiction, whether persons, property, business, or professions, it was secured in as ample a manner as it was before possessed.... The principle is conceded that the States can not rightfully tax the operations of the General Government. They can not tax the money of the Government deposited in the State banks, nor the agency of those banks in remitting it; but will any man maintain that their mere selection to perform this public service for the General Government would exempt the State banks and their ordinary business from State taxation? Had the United States, instead of establishing a bank at Philadelphia, employed a private banker to keep and transmit their funds, would it have deprived Pennsylvania of the right to tax his bank and his usual banking operations? It will not be pretended. Upon what principal, then, are the banking establishments of the Bank of the United States and their usual banking operations to be exempted from taxation? It is not their public agency or the deposits of the Government which the States claim a right to tax, but their banks and their banking powers, instituted and exercised within State jurisdiction for their private emolument—those powers and privileges for which they pay a bonus, and which the States tax in their own banks. The exercise of these powers within a State, no matter by

whom or under what authority, whether by private citizens in their original right, by corporate bodies created by the States, by foreigners or the agents of foreign governments located within their limits, forms a legitimate object of State taxation. From this and like sources, from the persons, property, and business that are found residing, located, or carried on under their jurisdiction, must the States, since the surrender of their right to raise a revenue from imports and exports, draw all the money necessary for the support of their governments and the maintenance of their independence. There is no more appropriate subject of taxation than banks, banking, and bank stocks, and none to which the States ought more pertinaciously to cling.

But Jackson did not stop here; from a constitutional standpoint, his most worrisome assertion concerned the larger principles of separation of powers and judicial review established a generation before in *Marbury v. Madison*. According to Jackson:

The Congress, the Executive, and the Court must each for itself be guided by its own opinion of the Constitution. Each public officer who takes an oath to support the Constitution swears that he will support it as he understands it, and not as it is understood by others. It is as much the duty of the House of Representatives, of the Senate, and of the President to decide upon the constitutionality of any bill or resolution which may be presented to them for passage or approval as it is of the supreme judges when it may be brought before them for judicial decision. The opinion of the judges has no more authority over Congress than the opinion of Congress has over the judges, and on that point the President is independent of both. The authority of the Supreme Court must not, therefore, be permitted to control the Congress or the Executive when acting in their legislative capacities, but to have only such influence as the force of their reasoning may deserve.

This assertion dovetailed with Jackson's attitude toward the Supreme Court throughout his presidency. As president, Jackson claimed that, "The authority of the Supreme Court must not, there-

fore, be permitted to control the Congress or the Executive," a principle he put into practice by forcibly removing Native Americans
from Georgia under the terms of the Indian Removal Act despite the
fact that the Supreme Court had ruled the law unconstitutional.[13]
Clay was quick to criticize Jackson's belief that "each public officer
may interpret the Constitution as he pleases," arguing that Jackson's
frequent use of the veto and rejection of judicial review amounted to
nullification in another guise. At one point during a speech to the
Senate, Clay rhetorically asked "what is the doctrine of the President
but that of South Carolina applied throughout the Union?"[14]

Beyond the legal and technical arguments, however, there was a
simple principle at the heart of the veto message that spoke volumes
about the Jacksonian worldview. According to Jackson:

> It is to be regretted that the rich and powerful too often bend the
> acts of government to their selfish purposes. Distinctions in socie-
> ty will always exist under every just government. Equality of tal-
> ents, of education, or of wealth can not be produced by human
> institutions. In the full enjoyment of the gifts of Heaven and the
> fruits of superior industry, economy, and virtue, every man is equal-
> ly entitled to protection by law; but when the laws undertake to
> add to these natural and just advantages artificial distinctions, to
> grant titles, gratuities, and exclusive privileges, to make the rich
> richer and the potent more powerful, the humble members of soci-
> ety—the farmers, mechanics, and laborers—who have neither the
> time nor the means of securing like favors to themselves, have a
> right to complain of the injustice of their Government. There are
> no necessary evils in government. Its evils exist only in its abuses.
> If it would confine itself to equal protection, and, as Heaven does
> its rains, shower its favors alike on the high and the low, the rich
> and the poor, it would be an unqualified blessing. In the act before
> me there seems to be a wide and unnecessary departure from these
> just principles.

Put another way, Jackson interpreted the Bank War as a conflict
between the haves and the have-nots, and he placed himself squarely in the latter's camp.

Interestingly, Jackson's veto message deviated from his previous public statements about the bank in one important respect. In his first and second annual messages, Jackson had indicated that he would ultimately leave the question of recharter in Congress's hands. Now, Congress had frustrated Jackson by rechartering the bank, so he changed his mind; rather than leave it to Congress to decide whether to recharter the bank, Jackson left the matter to his "fellow citizens," saying, "If sustained by my fellow citizens, I shall be grateful and happy; if not, I shall find in the motives which impel me ample grounds for contentment and peace."

Jackson's veto message is therefore the best and purest distillation of the Jacksonians' political, economic, social, and constitutional philosophy. Later, Jackson articulated a vision of the president as "the direct representative of the American People . . . elected by the People and responsible to them," a vision that made his actions the embodiment of the people's will.[15] Reflecting both his tendency to personalize political conflict and his instinctive view of political conflicts as fights between the forces of good and evil, Jackson claimed shortly after issuing the veto message, "instead of crushing me as was expected & intended, [the veto] will crush the Bank."[16] In other words, having now vetoed the bank's recharter, Jackson sought by his veto message to turn the election of 1832 into a referendum on the veto, seemingly playing into the hands of Clay, who believed that most voters did not share Jackson's anger toward the bank.

The reaction to Jackson's veto message, and its underlying philosophy, was swift and negative, at least in the Senate. Webster, who had opposed the bank's charter in 1815, claimed that Jackson had misused the veto, which was "an extraordinary power . . . [not] to be used in ordinary cases." He savaged Jackson's reasoning, saying "although Congress may have passed a law, and although the Supreme Court may have pronounced it constitutional, yet it is, nevertheless, no law at all, if he, in his good pleasure, sees fit to deny its effect, in other words, to repeal and annul it."[17] Calhoun also criticized Jackson's veto message, though he was not particularly committed to the bank per se, seeing the conflict between Jackson and Biddle only as an opportunity to help him into the presidency. As

BORN TO COMMAND.

OF VETO MEMORY.

HAD I BEEN CONSULTED.

KING ANDREW THE FIRST.

"King Andrew the First." One of the Whigs' main claims was that Jackson, by issuing so many vetoes, was acting as a king and disregarding the people's will (as expressed by Congress). This claim led to the Whig belief in the supremacy of Congress that was on of the main differences between the two parties. (*Library of Congress*)

one of Calhoun's political lieutenants noted, "if the defeat of General Jackson and the success of the Bank is to bring up Webster or Clay and with them the doctrines against which we have arrayed ourselves we will leave the Bank and General Jackson to fight out their own quarrels."[18] Aware of the fact that the Bank War was being co-opted by ambitious men for their own ends, Biddle lamented, "I have always deplored making the Bank a party question, but since the President will have it so, he must pay the penalty of his own rashness."[19]

Jackson's personalization of the bank issue was also connected to a stinging political defeat Clay and Calhoun had inflicted on the administration at roughly the same time: in February 1832, the Senate had defeated Van Buren's nomination to be minister to the Court of St. James's. Following Van Buren's resignation as secretary of state in 1831, Jackson named the New Yorker to the ambassadorial post as a recess appointment. But the appointment required confirmation by the Senate once it came back into session. Adding insult to injury, Calhoun—Jackson's own vice president—cast the deciding vote against Van Buren's nomination. That Van Buren had achieved some success in his brief tenure as ambassador seemed not to matter; Van Buren was known to be close to the president, and defeating his nomination was a shot across Jackson's bow.

Jackson's veto essentially signaled that the presidential election campaign had begun. The election of 1832 pitted Jackson and his hand-picked vice presidential nominee, Van Buren, against the National Republicans' Henry Clay and John Sergeant, a congressman from Pennsylvania and one of Biddle's personal friends. Jackson's veto of the bank's recharter, which his opponents claimed was symptomatic of the president's autocratic and tyrannical tendencies, became the election's main issue, and Biddle campaigned enthusiastically, spending thousands of dollars to reprint both Jackson's veto message and speeches denouncing the president. Jackson's supporters were outraged and concerned about Biddle's spending on the campaign. New York Senator William Marcy (he of "to the victor go the spoils" fame) noted, "The U.S. Bank is in the field and I cannot but fear the effect of 50 or 100 thousand dollars expended in conducting the election in a city such as New York."[20] Biddle's abandonment of political neutrality points to a larger irony in the Bank War, namely, due to his war on the bank, Jackson created the manipulative financial monster from which he claimed to be protecting the country. The campaign degenerated into a fight between competing stereotypes, with the Democrats painting the National Republicans as bought and paid for by corrupt money from the "golden vaults of the Mammoth Bank" while Clay attacked

Jackson's administration as a corrupt, antidemocratic tyranny characterized by "spoils, veto, and dictatorship."[21]

Ultimately, Jackson won reelection, but his share of the popular vote declined slightly, from 56 percent in 1828 to 54.2 percent. In other words, he had failed in his quest to improve his showing from four years earlier, a fact that he attributed to Biddle's decision to seek recharter before the election. On the other hand, Clay won only 38 percent of the vote (Anti-Mason candidate William Wirt got the other 7.8 percent), so Jackson interpreted his victory as a mandate to crush the bank. To do that, he decided to withdraw the federal government's money from the bank in the hope that doing so would starve it of funds and force it to close. Worse, from Biddle's perspective, was the fact that support for the bank among state bankers quickly ebbed following the election. Whatever their personal feelings about Jackson's policies, the president's reelection coupled with the fact that the Jacksonians had made the bank issue a test of party fidelity convinced many state bankers to support, or at least acquiesce to, the bank's demise. The state bankers' aversion to political participation coupled with fear about the consequences of defying the vindictive president led them to embrace what one historian has called "peace on the political front, not a bank war."[22] This was not paranoia on the bankers' part; defying the Democratic Party could have real, and painful, consequences. As John McFaul noted:

> Now that the president had committed himself and the Democratic party on the issue of a national bank, public statements on this issue were watched carefully for their political significance. Bankers might disclaim political interests but were very much aware of the reprisals and rewards from political action on both the state and national levels. A political blunder by a bank's directorate raised the possibility of counterattack by Democratic state legislators and financial neglect from the Treasury at Washington.[23]

At about this time, *Globe* editor Francis Blair complained to the president that Biddle was using "the money of the government for the purpose of breaking down the government," to which Jackson roared, "[Biddle] shan't have the public money. I'll remove the deposits."[24] In his annual message, delivered only a few weeks after the election, Jackson laid the groundwork for removing federal funds from the bank, saying:

> Such measures as are within the reach of the Secretary of the Treasury have been taken to enable him to judge whether the public deposits in that institution may be regarded as entirely safe; but as his limited power may prove inadequate to this object, I recommend the subject to the attention of Congress, under the firm belief that it is worthy of their serious investigation. An inquiry into the transactions of the institution, embracing the branches as well as the principal bank, seems called for by the credit which is given throughout the country to many serious charges impeaching its character, and which if true may justly excite the apprehension that it is no longer a safe depository of the money of the people.[25]

All the same, not everyone in the president's inner circle agreed about the wisdom of continuing the Bank War after the election or turning it into a litmus test of party identity. Newly inaugurated Vice President Van Buren, who had done so much to turn the bank into a political issue, now questioned the wisdom of delivering the final blow. Van Buren even tried to quiet Amos Kendall, whose editorials vociferously demanded that the president fulfill the voters' wishes and dispatch the bank, but with little success. Kendall merely turned his acid pen on Van Buren, warning the New Yorker that if he failed to toe the party line, "the party might have to turn away from him in 1836." Kendall's threat enraged Van Buren, who vocally upbraided the editor at the White House a few days later. Once it became clear that Kendall had Jackson's support, however, Van Buren backed down, though subsequent events vindicated his caution.[26]

Furthermore, many of Jackson's cabinet officers opposed removing the deposits. Worse from Old Hickory's perspective, on March 2, the House voted 109 to 46 against selling the government's share of the bank's stock, implicitly rejecting Jackson's aspersions on the institution's solvency. In response to these obstacles, Jackson raged against his enemies in Congress, most notably Clay and Calhoun. In a letter to a friend, Jackson complained that they wield the U. States Bank and with its corrupting influence they calculate to carry everything, even its recharter by two-thirds of Congress, against the veto of the executive, if they can do this, they calculate with certainty to put Clay or Calhoun in the Presidency—and I have no hesitation to say, if they can recharter the ban, with this hydra of corruption they will rule the nation, and its charter will be perpetual, and its corrupting influence destroy the liberty of our nation.[27]

Unburdened by self-reflection, Jackson was incapable of viewing opposition to his policies as anything other than evidence of corruption and a personal affront that demanded an aggressive response, so the administration's allies attacked journalists and politicians considered inadequately supportive of Jackson's policies. One example is Roger Taney's searing attack on the *New York Courier and Intelligencer*, a newspaper that had been Jackson's "warm friend" during the election but now opposed the president's policies toward the bank. According to Taney, this proved that the paper's editors "had received secretly from Mr. Biddle as President of the Bank fifty thousand dollars."[28] These attacks were highly effective: "Many of the supporters of Genl. Jackson who before had been favorable to the Bank now openly opposed it."[29] The Bank War had become the crucible of Democratic Party bona fides and, as a result, "a democrat had to be a Jacksonian," which meant strident opposition to the bank. [30]

Meanwhile, the administration was also dealing with a potentially explosive crisis over the tariff. The previous July, Jackson had signed into law the Tariff of 1832. This bill, written largely by former President John Quincy Adams in his new role as chairman of the House Committee on Manufactures, drastically reduced the tariff rates set under the 1828 "Tariff of Abominations." The Tariff of 1832 was supposed to remedy these concerns, but many Southerners felt the new bill did not reduce the tariff enough. A few days after vetoing the bank's recharter, Jackson signed the new tariff schedule into law. South Carolina, now represented in the

Senate by former Vice President Calhoun (the so-called mouth of the South), took the lead in resisting the new tariff, at least in part because Old Hickory supported it. In November 1832, a convention of nullifiers met in South Carolina and declared the tariffs of both 1828 and 1832 unenforceable in the state after February 1, 1833. Further, the convention took the provocative step of declaring that any federal attempt to coerce South Carolina to obey federal law would force the Palmetto State to secede from the union, a threat that took on additional urgency when Governor Robert Hayne established a force of more than twenty-five thousand men who would march to Charleston and repel a federal invasion.

In an attempt to calm South Carolina's fears, Jackson's fourth annual message contained a great deal of appeasing rhetoric designed to convince the South that the president intended no provocative action. For instance, on the tariff, Jackson recommended a reduction but placed the onus on Congress, saying:

> [T]he protection afforded by existing laws to any branches of the national industry should not exceed what may be necessary to counteract the regulations of foreign nations and to secure a supply of those articles of manufacture essential to the national independence and safety in time of war. If upon investigation it shall be found, as it is believed it will be, that the legislative protection granted to any particular interest is greater than is indispensably requisite for these objects, I recommend that it be gradually diminished, and that as far as may be consistent with these objects the whole scheme of duties be reduced to the revenue standard as soon as a just regard to the faith of the Government and to the preservation of the large capital invested in establishments of domestic industry will permit. . . . [T]hose who have vested their capital in manufacturing establishments can not expect that the people will continue permanently to pay high taxes for their benefit, when the money is not required for any legitimate purpose in the administration of the Government. . . . In some sections of the Republic its influence is deprecated as tending to concentrate wealth into a few hands, and as creating those germs of dependence and vice which in other countries have characterized the existence of monopolies

and proved so destructive of liberty and the general good. A large portion of the people in one section of the Republic declares it not only inexpedient on these grounds, but as disturbing the equal relations of property by legislation, and therefore unconstitutional and unjust. . . . Doubtless these effects are in a great degree exaggerated, and may be ascribed to a mistaken view of the considerations which led to the adoption of the tariff system; but they are never the less important in enabling us to review the subject with a more thorough knowledge of all its bearings upon the great interests of the Republic, and with a determination to dispose of it so that none can with justice complain.

A few paragraphs later, Jackson sketched a vision of the federal government: "Limited to a general superintending power to maintain peace at home and abroad, and to prescribe laws on a few subjects of general interest not calculated to restrict human liberty, but to enforce human rights, this Government will . . . [be] so simple and economical as scarcely to be felt."[31]

South Carolina's mobilization of troops, however, was a clear rejection of this fig leaf, and on December 10, in response to the nullification convention's declaration, Jackson issued a proclamation that took direct aim not only at armed resistance to federal law but to the idea of nullification. He wrote, "The ordinance is founded, not on the indefeasible right of resisting acts which are plainly unconstitutional, and too oppressive to be endured, but on the strange position that any one State may not only declare an act of Congress void, but prohibit its execution." Noting that the logical end of nullification could only be the Union's destruction, Jackson said, "I consider, then, the power to annul a law of the United States, assumed by one State, *incompatible with the existence of the Union, contradicted expressly by the letter of the Constitution, unauthorized by its spirit, inconsistent with every principle on which It was founded, and destructive of the great object for which it was formed.*" Reminding South Carolinians that, "There is no settled design to oppress you," he went on to warn them, "The laws of the United States must be executed. I have no discretionary power on the subject—my duty is emphatically pronounced in the Constitution. Those who told you that you might peaceably prevent their execution, deceived you—they could not have been deceived themselves. They know that a forcible opposition could alone prevent the execution of the laws, and they know that such opposition must be repelled. Their object is disunion, but be not deceived by names; disunion, by armed force, is TREASON." He then called the nullifiers, "the authors of the first attack on the Constitution of your country," and threatened, "You may disturb [the country's] peace—you may interrupt the course of its prosperity—you may cloud its reputation for stability— but its tranquility will be restored, its prosperity will return, and the stain upon its national character will be transferred and remain an eternal blot on the memory of those who caused the disorder."[32]

In short, Jackson told South Carolina that any attempt to prevent the execution of federal law within the state would provoke a swift and decisive reaction from the federal government. To make this threat credible, on March 2, at Jackson's urging, Congress passed the Force Bill, which gave the president the authority to deploy federal troops to South Carolina to compel the enforcement of federal law.

The president's proclamation and the Force Bill were vintage Jackson: bold, pugnacious, and uncompromising. Yet behind the scenes, the administration scrambled to find a compromise that gave both sides the ability to claim victory while averting the need for bloodshed. The obvious answer was to change the law in such a way that South Carolina no longer objected, allowing the administration to claim that it upheld its principles while at the same time removing the source of the conflict. The answer came from Jackson's two main antagonists—Clay and Calhoun—who proposed what came to be known as the Compromise Tariff, which gradually lowered tariff rates over the next decade and included some other provisions designed to lower prices and thereby appease South Carolina's nullifiers. Congress overwhelmingly passed the new tariff, the House voting 119 to 85, the Senate 29 to 16. Once Jackson signed the new tariff, Calhoun rushed the text to Charleston, where on March 11 a second nullification convention repealed the earlier secession ordinance (though, in an attempt to save face, it did nullify the now unnecessary Force Bill). Though Jackson's proclamation and the Force Bill certainly provided the stick, historians generally regard Clay and Calhoun's carrot as the crucial step in ending the nullification crisis.

O nce the danger of civil war abated, Jackson could again turn his attention to prosecuting his war against the Bank of the United States, which he did with gusto. In 1833, Jackson had told Van Buren "we have the Bank now check mated . . . [and] will treat her gently if she behaves."[33] Behaving, however, was the furthest thing from Biddle's mind. During the nullification crisis, Biddle asked Daniel Webster to try to reason with the president over the deposits, apparently believing that as long as he could keep the bank in business, a second opportunity for recharter might present itself. Biddle's efforts came to naught, however; even if Jackson had had no deep-seated aversion to banks or questions about the bank's constitutionality, he considered Biddle's actions during the recent election as a personal insult that demanded a response. As the events leading up to the recharter fight make clear, Jackson had a tendency to personalize political struggles, thereby ensuring that he would not be satisfied merely defeating the bank; he had to kill it. However, there were also practical reasons to do so. Writing to Jackson at the end of February 1833, James Hamilton advised the president that the bank still had the means to cause the administration trouble. Hamilton feared that Biddle would curtail lending or manipulate the currency exchange rates in order to "induce a strong feeling in favor of a recharter of the Bank as the only means of restoring a sound currency." Francis Blair, editor of the *Globe* and a respected member of Jackson's Kitchen Cabinet was blunter: he advised the president that "the damned Bank ought to be put down" and the only way to do that was "to take from it the whole of the public money."[34]

Unfortunately for the president, most of his cabinet, including Treasury Secretary McLane, opposed this policy. Under the bank's charter, only the Treasury secretary could remove the federal government's deposits from the bank, so Jackson needed McLane's assent, but the president was destined for disappointment. McLane opposed removing the deposits before the bank's charter expired in March 1836, and, given the federal government's experiences during the mid-1810s, the idea of placing the Treasury's money in state banks made him uneasy. On May 20, McLane wrote a letter to Jackson outlining his concerns and refusing to remove the deposits. Jackson should not have been surprised by McLane's defiance; after all, according to Taney, from the beginning "it was well understood that McLane was in favor of a renewal of the [bank's] charter; and . . . this opinion was known to the President before he appointed [McLane] to the Treasury Department."[35]

That Jackson would knowingly appoint to his cabinet someone who disagreed with him on such a seemingly important issue may strike readers as foolhardy and therefore unlikely, but it points to the fact that the Democrats at this point were not a political party in the sense of having a defined agenda or a coherent set of policy goals that united them. At the 1832 Democratic national nominating convention, the party had not adopted a platform; it had only nominated Jackson and Van Buren for president and vice president. Aside from patronage, it was fidelity to Jackson, rather than any core set of beliefs or policies, that held the party together, and as result people who identified themselves as members of "the democracy" held a broad range of views on issues. The Bank War, by creating a test of party identity, melded the party together, but the diversity of opinion represented by Jackson's cabinet members demonstrates that this process was far from complete; Jackson needed to purge the dissenters from his cabinet.

Thus, left with few options, Jackson shuffled his cabinet: Secretary of State Livingston became US minister to France, and McLane took over the State Department. The president then appointed William J. Duane to be secretary of the Treasury, effective June 1. Duane was an Irish-born Philadelphia lawyer who, almost twenty years earlier, had defeated Biddle in the latter's bid for reelection to the Pennsylvania legislature. That, coupled with Duane's vehement opposition to the bank, made him the ideal candidate for the Treasury Department, at least as far as Jackson was concerned, though Jackson soon came to rue the appointment. On July 20, the president asked Duane to appoint Amos Kendall, a member of Jackson's Kitchen Cabinet who was largely responsible for drafting Jackson's first five annual messages to Congress, a special agent whose sole responsibility was to identify state banks to take on the federal government deposits once they were removed from the Bank of the United States. Duane obliged, but Jackson was disappointed when Kendall, after speaking with state bankers in Boston, New York,

William Duane. (*Library of Congress*)

Philadelphia, and Baltimore, recommended not removing the funds from the Bank of the United States, at least not before its charter expired. It was a moment when pragmatism triumphed over ideology, and therefore should have given Jackson pause, but true to form, the president pressed ahead with his plan to strangle the bank.

At a cabinet meeting on September 17, Jackson announced his decision to remove the federal government's deposits from the Bank of the United States. During the course of the discussion, McLane vehemently opposed this policy, as did Secretary of War Lewis Cass and Secretary of the Navy Levi Woodbury, while Attorney General Taney supported the move. Treasury Secretary Duane urged the president to wait until Congress returned to session in December, and, having heard his cabinet members' opinions, Jackson adjourned the meeting and asked the men to return the following day. At the next meeting, Jackson asked Taney to read a report on the federal deposits that the attorney general had prepared. Taney called the Bank of the United States "a Government which has gradually increased in strength from the day of its establishment. The question between it and the people has become one of power—a question which its adherents do not scruple to avow must ultimately be decided in favor of the Bank."[36] Taney recited an exhaustive list of the bank's misdeeds (real and imagined), even bringing up Biddle's impolitic handling of the French spoliation claims in 1831. It was a virtuoso performance that left few in doubt of the president's next move.

Following Taney's peroration, and as if he was following a script, Jackson exclaimed, "How shall we answer to God, our country, or ourselves, if we permit the public money to be thus used to corrupt the people?"[37] He then instructed Duane to begin removing the deposits. Though Jackson said he would accept all responsibility for having the deposit removal, Duane refused. In a letter Duane sent to Jackson on September 21, the Treasury secretary argued that removing the deposits from the Bank of the United States and placing the money in what he called "local and irresponsible banks" would have a disastrous effect on public confidence. Duane hated the Bank of the United States—he went to great lengths to make that clear in his letter to Jackson—but, at the moment, he saw the bank as the lesser of two evils.[38] Aghast, Jackson demanded Duane's resignation, but he refused and said he would not move the government's money until Congress came into session that December. Jackson tried to reason with Duane, at one point reminding him of his promise to "retire if we could not finally agree," to which Duane replied that he had made that promise "indiscreetly." Jackson then tried to convince Duane that because the Treasury secretary was an executive agent, he had a responsibility to follow the president's orders or resign. Duane countered that in casting the bank's charter the way it had, Congress had conferred on the Treasury secretary a "discretionary power" that extended beyond Jackson's expectation that his cabinet secretary would follow orders.[39]

In that sense, Duane had history on his side. Though it will surely strike modern readers as unusual that a cabinet member refused the president's direct order and expected to retain his place, as historian Donald Cole noted, "cabinet officers at the time had become accustomed to considerable independence."[40] In the history of the Republic up to that point, only John Adams had ever fired members of his cabinet (Secretary of State Timothy Pickering and Secretary of War James McHenry in 1800), and the backlash was so intense that it reinforced the perception that cabinet members were essentially independent actors and not answerable to the president. To

Jackson, who was always alert to perceived slights to the office of the president or to his ability to control the government, this was nonsense; having
appointed Duane (even knowing that the
Treasury secretary disagreed with him),
Old Hickory expected loyalty.

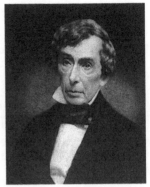

Roger B. Taney. (*Library of Congress*)

Nevertheless, Duane remained
adamant that he would not remove the
funds, and Jackson did not suffer frustration quietly. He had already suffered
through one cabinet implosion—the first
time that had ever happened in American
history—and was reluctant to endure the
political costs of a second one. But having no other options, on
September 23, Jackson sent Duane a terse note that said his "further
services as Secretary of the Treasury are no longer required."[41] Of
Duane, Jackson would later complain, "he is either the weakest mortal, or the most strange composition I have ever met with."[42]

Needing a Treasury secretary who would unquestioningly follow
his orders to remove the deposits, Jackson appointed Attorney
General Taney to the position. Taney, an old man by the standards
of the day (he was fifty-six), was a staunch Jacksonian who had
briefly acted as Jackson's secretary of war following John Eaton's
departure from the cabinet in 1831. Taney had been the only cabinet member to recommend vetoing the bank's recharter. What made
Taney particularly attractive as a Treasury secretary was his background in banking: he was a personal friend of Union Bank of
Maryland President Thomas Ellicott's (the man Langdon Cheves
wanted to succeed him as president of the Bank of the United States
in 1823) and had made a considerable amount of money investing in
Ellicott's bank. In addition, Ellicott's antagonism toward the Bank of
the United States—born of having been denied the institution's
presidency and some conflicts the Union Bank had with the Bank of
the United States over bank note redemptions—had rubbed off on
Taney.[43]

Taney did not share Duane and McLane's qualms about removing the government's money from the Bank of the United States and was eager to deliver the deathblow to the bank. Crucially, Taney's appointment as Treasury secretary was a recess appointment, meaning he could only hold the position until Congress came back into session and confirmed the nomination. This had to occur before the end of the congressional session or the position would again be vacant, so Taney had to move quickly. Almost immediately, Taney issued a proclamation that beginning October 1, all federal government receipts would be directed to seven state banks identified by Kendall: Boston's Commonwealth Bank and Merchants Bank; New York's Bank of Manhattan Company, the Bank of America, and the Mechanics Bank; Philadelphia's Girard Bank; and Baltimore's Union Bank of Maryland (in which Taney was a stockholder). Most of the banks Kendall selected were viewed as reliably Jacksonian, and most historians have seen political considerations at work in the selection of these pet banks.

Though new government revenue would flow into the pet banks, Taney announced that the Treasury Department would continue issuing drafts against the Bank of the United States in order to draw down its accounts. Taney's announcement caused a 1.5 percent drop in the bank's stock, and by December most of the federal government's money was gone. The *Boston Post*, a Jacksonian newspaper, mockingly proclaimed the bank's epitaph: "Biddled, Diddled, and Undone."[44] In his fifth annual message to Congress, Jackson attacked the Bank of the United States as "a permanent electioneering engine" and justified his removal of the federal government's money on the grounds that:

> The near approach of the day on which the [bank's] charter will expire, as well as the conduct of the bank, appeared to me to call for this measure upon the high considerations of public interest and public duty. The extent of its misconduct, however, although known to be great, was not at that time fully developed by proof. It was not until late in the month of August that I received from the Government directors an official report establishing beyond question that this great and powerful institution had been actively

"The Downfall of Mother Bank." A pro-administration cartoon celebrating the president's decision to remove federal deposits from the Bank of the United States, portending "the downfall of the party engine and corrupt monopoly." Biddle, Clay, Webster, and the Devil are all depicted as fleeing the collapsing ban while a jubilant citizen looks on. (*Library of Congress*)

engaged in attempting to influence the elections of the public officers by means of its money, and that, in violation of the express provisions of its charter, it had by a formal resolution placed its funds at the disposition of its president to be employed in sustaining the political power of the bank.[45]

Philip Hone blasted the message in his diary, calling its language "violent and intemperate . . . [and] undignified."[46] The bank's supporters in Congress struck back. On December 26, Clay claimed that removal of the deposits amounted to "a revolution, hitherto bloodless, but rapidly tending towards a total change of the pure Republican character of the Government, and to the concentration of power in the hands of one man."[47] Ironically, though Clay was speaking of Jackson, these words could easily have been used by Jackson to denounce Biddle and the bank, a reflection of the degree to which partisanship and ideology had strangled pragmatism and common sense.

Almost from the beginning, the removal of the deposits was a fias-co. Jackson's announcement sent shock waves through the financial community. Hone noted that by the middle of November, "Stocks of every description have fallen. . . . Money cannot be had on bond and mortgage at seven per cent., and I am told good notes will hardly be discounted at nine per cent."[48] In an attempt to hedge against retal-iatory action by the bank, Taney prepared drafts in the amounts of $500,000 and $100,000 that he sent to at least two of the pets; if Biddle tried to ruin these banks by aggressively redeeming their notes, the banks could present the drafts and replenish their specie reserves.[49] Naturally, and with what one historian has called "inde-cent haste," the banks quickly redeemed the drafts, violating the unwritten rule that the government would notify the bank when large liabilities were coming due, demonstrating that the Treasury Department could not control the pets.[50]

Worse, individuals close to the administration, including the shifty Reuben Whitney (a Philadelphia banker and occasional mem-ber of the Kitchen Cabinet), profited on their advance knowledge of Jackson's actions by short selling shares of Bank of the United States stock. When the price of the bank's stock fell in response to the administration's decision to remove federal deposits, Whitney and other friends of the administration made a tidy profit, though their unsavory behavior was soon exposed in newspapers friendly to the bank.[51] That was far from the only scandal resulting from the removal of the deposits. Because the Treasury secretary was ulti-mately responsible for selecting banks to hold federal deposits, there were no standards regarding what institutions might qualify for gov-ernment funds, and the administration had every incentive to use the funds to reward state banks owned by supporters. On the one hand, the Treasury Department told the pet banks that it expected the fed-eral deposits to "afford increased facilities to the commercial and other classes of the community, and the department anticipates from you the adoption of such a course . . . as will prove acceptable to the people and safe to the Government," but on the other hand, mem-bers of the administration called for the selection of banks that were friendly to the administration, and Kendall predicted "those [banks] which are in hands politically friendly will be preferred."[52]

Once Treasury Department revenue began flowing into the Union Bank of Maryland, its president, Thomas Ellicott, started using the funds for a variety of harebrained speculations that quickly went south. When Ellicott could no longer hide the bank's losses, he pressured Taney to deposit more government revenue in the Union Bank. The Treasury secretary complained of Ellicott's "cool, calculating duplicity with which he was tormenting me for his own private gain" and was further embarrassed when Ellicott tried to solicit funds from the Bank of the United States. Taney responded viciously the following year, recalling in his memoir that he "united with a majority of the [Union Bank of Maryland's] stockholders in electing a Board of Directors opposed to [Ellicott's] reelection as President of the Bank." Taney gloated in his memoirs that this move had earned him Ellicott's "deep resentment," but whatever joy he may have felt in victory was short-lived: the Union Bank of Maryland failed soon after, leading to a bitter series of public charges and countercharges that only embarrassed Taney, Ellicott, and the president.[53]

The debacle in Baltimore quickly became a political liability for the administration, with anti-Jacksonian forces in Congress led by Henry Clay demanding investigations into Taney's choice of pet banks. Clay charged—correctly, as it turned out—that Taney owned shares in Ellicott's bank, and the Treasury secretary was forced to divulge that on the day that federal money was deposited in the Union Bank of Maryland, he owned shares in the bank worth approximately $5,000. While Taney escaped any official sanction for his actions, Clay's investigation nonetheless seemed to confirm the suspicion that the removal of federal deposits from the Bank of the United States—and, by extension, the Bank War itself—was motivated more by an attempt to win spoils than any desire to free the United States from the clutches of the "monster Bank."

Worse, in Philadelphia, almost half of the city's banks refused to even discuss the possibility of taking on federal deposits, a fact that many in the administration ascribed to Biddle's influence. Kendall tried to interest the Bank of Pennsylvania in accepting the deposits because of that institution's connection to the Keystone State's political leaders, but its directors refused and Taney instead selected the Girard Bank. Initially, things went smoothly, but when word of Ellicott's peculations threatened to sour public opinion on the pet bank scheme, the Girard Bank's stockholders voted to annul the institution's contract with the Treasury and to refuse any further federal government deposits. Though only a temporary move (the bank was later reappointed as a pet), the Girard Bank's actions were nonetheless another well-publicized rebuke to the Jackson administration. For his part, Jackson responded with characteristic pugnacity, swearing that he would never return the deposits to the Bank of the United States, promising that the funds "would stay in collectors' strongboxes if no state banks accepted them."[54]

Jackson's temper tantrum may have been ideologically satisfying, but such rhetoric failed to address the havoc that the removal of the deposits and their placement in the unruly state banks had wreaked on the country's finances. Worse, the federal government's drafts on the Bank of the United States quickly depleted the bank's reserves of federal money. On December 13, 1833, the Treasury Department notified the pet banks that it would soon begin issuing drafts against *their* reserves of federal funds; the party was over and they could not loan against what they assumed to be the limitless stores of Treasury specie held in the Bank of the United States. Taney failed to give the pet banks any warning of this change in administration policy, so they in turn immediately curtailed lending in order to have the funds on hand to redeem the Treasury Department's drafts, choking the economy of credit.[55] The pet banks' reaction to the administration's actions was entirely predictable, but it threatened a political disaster. If the country went into recession so quickly after the administration implemented its financial agenda, the voters would blame the Democrats. Fearing a political backlash, the Treasury Department adopted a contradictory approach to dealing with the pet banks: on the one hand, it pressured them to increase their lending, but on the other hand, fearful that the banks would collapse and *that* would embarrass the president, it encouraged the banks to increase their specie.

Nor was this the only case where the Treasury Department's ideological war against the Bank of the United States contributed to

"The Political Barbecue." An anti-administration political cartoon depicting Jackson as a
dead is being roasted over the flames of public opinion. Standing behind Jackson, Clay,
Webster, and Biddle discuss the removal of the deposits, while Van Buren (depicted as a pig)
sneaks away carrying a sack of Treasury notes. (*Library of Congress*)

contradictory policy imperatives. The department heavily discour-
aged the issuance of bank notes in denominations under twenty dollars, which historian Harry N. Scheiber called one prong of "a much
broader attack by the administration on the 'paper money system' as
it then existed."[56] In March 1835, the Treasury Department forbid
the pets from accepting any notes under five dollars in payment of
debts to the federal government, and then raised the ban to any note
under ten dollars beginning in March 1836.[57] This move was
designed to achieve two goals: appease the politically influential
hard-money men, who demanded the total elimination of paper
money as a circulating medium and limit the Treasury Department's
liability in guaranteeing the pets' bank notes by curtailing the number and total value of notes in circulation. The administration's pro-
pagandist, Francis Blair, asserted in the *Globe* that this was the ideal
compromise because "for large transactions and commercial purposes Banks and Bank paper should be permitted to exist. The evils
of banking would be thus curtailed, and its risks thrown upon that

part of society which profits by it, and is most able to bear occasional losses."[58]

At the same time, the need for a national currency, which the Bank of the United States had provided, meant that the Treasury Department needed the pet banks to accept each other's notes at face value. The pets were skeptical of accepting one another's notes at par, particularly after Ellicott's speculations with Treasury funds almost bankrupted the Union Bank of Maryland. Whatever the state banks' concerns, politics demanded that they accept each other's notes at face value; after all, one of Jackson's major complaints about the bank was that it had (allegedly) failed to create a national currency. It was thus not *politically* acceptable for the pet banks to discount each other's notes, whatever the merits of the *economic* reasons for doing so. Consequently, Taney was forced to guarantee the various pets' notes, thereby creating an incentive for the pets to increase their issuance of notes. The pet banks reasoned that if they ran into problems and could not redeem the notes in specie, the Treasury Department would provide the necessary funds in order to protect them.

Taney's actions are a perfect example of what economists call moral hazard, or a situation where one individual or group is encouraged to take risks because someone else is bearing the cost of those risks. In this case, the administration got a national currency but at the cost of taking on the risk that the state banks would be unable (or unwilling) to redeem their notes at face value. When Levi Woodbury replaced Taney as secretary of the Treasury in July 1834, he almost immediately rescinded the department's guarantee of the pets' bank notes, calling the policy "questionable in principle," but was soon forced, reluctantly, to change course and return to Taney's policy.[59]

At the same time, Jackson had problems with the extreme hard-money wing of the Democratic Party, for whom the removal of the deposits did not go far enough. For men like Benton, removing the federal government's money from the Bank of the United States did nothing to cure what they saw as the most important illness in the American economic system, namely, its reliance on paper money rather than specie. In fact, neither Taney, for all of his hostility to the

Bank of the United States, nor his successor as secretary of the Treasury, Levi Woodbury, were advocates of hard money. Both men believed it was the overissuance of paper money, not paper money itself, that caused instability in the banking system, and they only went so far as to support legislation prohibiting the issuance of small notes, not all emissions of paper.[60]

This enraged the extreme hard-money wing of the Jacksonian coalition, which believed the administration was selling out a core article of its economic agenda.[61] Jackson's election had provoked a torrent of proposals designed to restrict or even eliminate emissions of paper currency. In 1832, the House debated a resolution that would have taxed small bank notes and prevented the United States from accepting notes below five dollars; though the resolution did not pass, it nonetheless demonstrates many Americans' antipathy toward paper money. However, the more extreme elements of Jackson's Democratic coalition were restless, feeling that the president had not gone far enough. Destroying the Bank of the United States was all well and good, they argued, but in so doing the administration had failed to demonetize paper and disconnect the federal government entirely from the banking system.[62]

To the hard-money men's horror, Jackson's assault on the bank, if anything, more firmly entrenched paper money in the American economy, and, given the fact that the Treasury Department was now guaranteeing the pet banks' notes, the federal government was more involved with the banking sector than ever. Treasury Department rules forbidding pet banks from accepting low-denomination notes for payment of public debts in 1835 and 1836 did not mollify these hard-money men, who demanded a pure economy denuded of paper money. This politically influential faction could not be ignored and would not be placated by half-measures, seeing the Bank War as the basis for a new party system composed of "a hard money party against a paper money party."[63] In a sense, Benton got his wish: the Democrats' hard money faction coalesced into a faction of the party known as the "locofoco" that essentially silenced more moderate voices in the party. Ralph Waldo Emerson described the locofocos as the "new race," claiming they were "stiff, heady, and rebellious; they are fanatics in freedom; they hate tolls, taxes, turn-pikes, banks, hierarchies, governors, yea, almost all laws." Their emergence, and the power they exercised within the party, was the final triumph of ideology over pragmatism.

Having abandoned political neutrality, Biddle declared war on the Jackson administration and vowed to hoist the president on his own economic petard. On July 30, Biddle provocatively told the New York branch of the Bank of the United States that he intended to "crush the Kitchen Cabinet," and in a February letter to his friend Joseph Hopkinson, Biddle expressed his defiance of Jackson, say-ing, "This worthy President thinks that because he has scalped Indians and imprisoned Judges, he is to have his way with the Bank. He is mistaken."[64] Biddle's letter to Hopkinson is interesting because it reflects the fact that by February 1833, the Bank War had become personal for Biddle. Gone were the high-minded statements about political neutrality and the need to do what was best for the country. Biddle had personalized the Bank War in much the same way as Jackson; it had now become the fight to the death that Jackson had predicted in summer 1832 when he accused the bank of trying to kill him.

In response to the administration's concerted attack on the bank, Biddle made a fateful decision: he would contract the money supply in the hope that the resulting recession would force the Jackson administration to change direction. Triggering a recession was an incredibly risky gambit because it would vindicate Jackson's claims about the bank's undue power and influence. It is a measure of Biddle's desperation that he was willing to run this risk in order to save the bank. Biddle laid out his strategy in a letter to a friend in January 1834, claiming, "the ties of party allegiance can only be bro-ken by the actual conviction of existing distress in the community. Nothing but the evidence of suffering abroad will produce any effect in Congress."[65] The Bank of the United States had actually begun contracting its loans following Jackson's veto, but by the end of 1833, Biddle had gained additional leverage owing to the fact that as state banks received federal deposits, they issued more loans, paid in their own bank notes; these notes circulated through the economy, eventually making their way to the Bank of the United States. These notes represented a liability for the state banks—in this case, a debt that needed to be paid in specie if the note was ever presented to the issuing bank—giving the Bank of the United States leverage over the state banks. By redeeming the state bank notes, the Bank of the United States lowered the amount of specie these banks held, which in turn lowered the amount of money they could loan and thereby lowered the total number of bank notes in circulation.

The Bank of the United States did not loan money against the specie it held; during the last quarter of 1833, the bank embraced what one historian called a "scorched-earth policy," cutting its lending by $5.5 million, thereby increasing its specie reserve by 34 percent from June 1833 to August 1834.[66] The effect of Biddle's credit contraction was magnified by the compromise tariff that Congress had passed to end the nullification crisis. Before 1833, merchants could postpone paying the tariff until after they had sold the goods they imported, but the Compromise Tariff of 1833 mandated payment at the time of importation. This change increased merchants' need for short-term credit at just the moment when banks were not lending. The sudden recession spurred widespread violence; by one count, the country was rocked by nearly 150 riots over economic issues in 1835 alone.[67] Finally, small-denomination coins had all but disappeared from circulation. Despite an inflow of silver from South America that was coined at the US Mint during the early 1820s, specie was scarce; most of the new silver coins were exported to Asia, and day-to-day transactions were conducted using worn Spanish coins. Specie was so scarce that gold coins circulated at a premium of 4 to 10 percent (meaning they were worth more than their face value), and at least one historian has estimated that coins minted from precious metal accounted for less than 11 percent of the total money in circulation.[68] The result of all of these developments was that money and credit were harder to come by, and by the fourth quarter of 1833, the United States was in a recession and scarcely any region in the country was spared business failures.

The pet banks were caught flat-footed by Biddle's credit contraction. A group of New York bankers was forced to admit to Treasury

Secretary Taney that they owed the Bank of the United States $1 million and their share of the government deposits was not enough to keep them solvent. Taney told the bankers to be more careful in making loans and not to redeem drafts presented by the Bank of the United States. In other words, Taney advised these bankers to suspend specie payments, albeit on a limited scale, while simultaneously begging them to increase lending.[69] When a group of New York bankers traveled to Washington to complain to the president about the financial difficulties they were experiencing and ask for some relief, Jackson dismissed the men, condescendingly saying, "Insolvent do you say? What do you come to me for, then? Go to Nicholas Biddle. We have no money here, gentlemen. He has millions of specie in his vaults, at this moment, lying idle, and yet you come to *me* to save you from breaking. I tell you, gentlemen, it's all politics."[70] That was certainly true, but it was little comfort to the thousands of Americans struggling to support themselves.

When Congress reassembled in December for the so-called Panic Congress—a name given because of the general discord in the economy—the bank's congressional supporters in the Senate struck back against the president. Prior to the election of 1832, Jacksonian and anti-Jacksonian forces had been evenly balanced in the Senate. In the newly elected twenty-third Congress, however, the anti-Jacksonian forces held twenty-six seats to the Jacksonians' twenty-two. Although the House, which was controlled by Jacksonians, generally supported the president, the upper chamber became a thorn in his side. Diarist Philip Hone observed, "In both Houses of Congress, the all-absorbing topic of the removal of the deposits occupies the time, and the members on both sides of the question seem determined to have their talk out."[71] On December 10, Henry Clay offered a resolution requesting that Jackson turn over the statements made to the cabinet before the president decided to remove the federal government's deposits from the bank. When Jackson refused, citing executive privilege, Clay took off the gloves. On February 5, he orchestrated the passage of two Senate resolutions. The first called Taney's reasons for removing federal government deposits from the bank "unsatisfactory and insufficient," but the second was more significant.

Under Clay's leadership, and after a heated ten-week debate, the Senate voted 26 to 20 to censure the president. According to the censure resolution, "in taking upon himself the responsibility of removing the deposits of the public money from the Bank of the U. States, the President of the U. S. has assumed the exercise of a power over the Treasury of the U. States, not provided to him by the Constitution and laws, and dangerous to the liberties of the people." Though in 1800, Congressman Edward Livingston (who later became Jackson's secretary of state) introduced a motion of censure against John Adams, the House did not pass the motion. Therefore, Jackson was the first president censured, and when he tried to explain his actions in a message to the Senate dated April 15, the Senate voted not to receive the message and ordered that it not be recorded in its journal.[72] Nor was the censure motion the end of the matter. In June 1834, the Senate, by a vote of 28 to 18, rejected Taney's nomination as secretary of the Treasury. This was the first time in US history that the Senate rejected a presidential cabinet appointment. It was a stark reminder of how bitter and personal the Bank War had become and a chilling reminder of the costs of ideological intransigence and partisan games.

Jackson's response to the Senate's censure was filled with his characteristic mix of defiance and self-righteousness. Claiming that, "Without notice, unheard and untried, I thus find myself charged on the records of the Senate, and in a form hitherto unknown in our history, with the high crime of violating the laws and Constitution of my country," Jackson attacked the Senate's authority to censure him, saying, "That the Senate possesses a high judicial power and that instances may occur in which the President of the United States will be amenable to it is undeniable; but under the provisions of the Constitution it would seem to be equally plain that neither the President nor any other officer can be rightfully subjected to the operation of the judicial power of the Senate except in the cases and under the forms prescribed by the Constitution." Jackson then defended his actions, claiming that Congress had passed no law mandating that public money be deposited in the Bank of the United States and reserving to the secretary of the Treasury the right to determine where to house the government's funds.[73]

The statement was vintage Jackson: pugnacious, combative, and uncompromising, and as a consequence it only fueled the conflict. Hone decried Jackson's "hostility against the Senate," which he predicted would lead the president "into some extravagant acts of rage, which he relies upon his popularity to bear him out of."[74] Hone was prophetic. Soon after reconvening, the Senate rejected Jackson's nominations for bank directors, a clear challenge to the president's authority. Because Jackson relied on the directors for information about Biddle's activities, he considered it essential to have his appointments confirmed by the Senate. In May, Jackson nominated the same men, and that same month, the Senate rejected the nominations by a lopsided 30 to 11 vote. Uncharacteristically cowed by the Senate's action, Jackson reluctantly nominated less-controversial choices who were quickly approved, and he held back on nominations for other government positions until later in the session.[75]

Though the Senate was taking the fight to Jackson, Biddle was losing the battle for public opinion and, with it, the Bank War. In February 1834, George Wolf, the Democratic governor of Pennsylvania, who had up to this point been a strong supporter of the bank, attacked Biddle for having wrought "indiscriminate ruin" on the Keystone State. Shortly thereafter, Pennsylvania's Senate passed a resolution that denounced the bank's contractionary financial policies, and the state's two senators, William Wilkins and Samuel Kean, publicly announced they would no longer support the Bank of the United States. In New York, Governor William Marcy also attacked Biddle for the economic damage to that state's banks and pushed a bill through the legislature authorizing him to loan state banks New York state stock. Even Biddle's friends were getting nervous about the costs of the economic downturn he had engineered. In February, a group of bankers friendly to Biddle and Bank of the United States formed the Union Committee, the sole purpose of which was to convince Biddle to change course and end the contraction. The committee's entreaties displeased Biddle, and he vented that frustration in a letter to Pennsylvania Congressman Samuel Breck, writing:

"General Jackson Slyaing the Many Headed Monster." A classic pro-administration depiction of Jacksonians' belief that teh Bank of the United States was a "many headed monster" that needed to be slain. (*Library of Congress*)

A committee from New York has been visiting the Bank for the purpose of procuring some relief for that city. . . . Yesterday the Board was to have decided it, & I have no doubt that the Bank would have made an effort to give relief—but when we saw [Pennsylvania Governor George Wolf's] message—saw how totally useless the efforts of the Bank had been to sustain the credit of the State in appeasing the spirit of party—and how little reliance could be placed on the men in power, we determined that it was in vain to make an effort—and accordingly, instead of sending the relief expected, we wrote to the New York Committee that the conduct of the Governor of Pennsylvania obliged the Bank to look to its own safety, and therefore we declined doing anything at present.[76]

Though he certainly would not have recognized this fact, Biddle had become what he most detested about Jackson: a partisan making policy decisions that carried enormous repercussions based on

whim, emotion, and personal feeling. He was no longer the politically neutral technocrat slavishly devoted to the nation's interest, a fact
driven home in a letter Biddle wrote in March 1834. According to
Biddle, "by removing the public revenues, [Jackson] has relieved
the Bank from all responsibility for the currency, and imposed upon
it a necessity to look primarily to the interests of the Stockholders
committed to our charge. Our friends must therefore bear with us, if
in the midst of the present troubles, we should endeavor to strength-
en the Bank so as to make it able here after to interpose effectively for
the relief of the County."[77] In another letter Biddle wrote, "If the
bank remains strong and quiet, the course of events will save the
bank, and save all institutions of the country which are now in peril.
But, if from too great sensitiveness, from a fear of offending, or the
desire of conciliating, the bank permits itself to be frightened or
coaxed into any relaxation of its present measures, the relief will
itself be cited as evidence that the measures of the government are
not injurious or oppressive, and the bank will inevitably be prostrat-
ed."[78]

In his all-out war on the bank, Jackson was determined to win, no
matter the cost, and he, too, resorted to inflicting economic pain on
Americans in order to win the battle for public opinion. In January
1834, Jackson ordered Secretary of War Lewis Cass to demand that
the Bank of the United States stop paying Revolutionary War veterans' pensions and immediately return the money, along with all of
the records relating to the payments, to the federal government. The
administration had tried this tactic on a limited scale with the
Portsmouth branch in 1829, but now it applied to all of the bank's
branches. Biddle refused to comply with the order, citing the fact
that the bank was legally obligated to pay the pensions, at least until
its charter expired in 1836. Expecting this response, Cass ordered
all pension payments suspended immediately. Cynically, the president had concluded that the Revolutionary War veterans would
blame the bank rather than the administration for the suspension of
pension payments, further eroding public support for Biddle's bank.
To make sure no one missed the point, Jackson turned over to
Congress Biddle's refusal to return the pension money and records,

adding for good measure that the bank "not only defied the government but inflicted misery on patriotic Americans who had fought bravely for their country and were now repaid with arrogant contempt."[79] The House referred Jackson's complaint to Polk's Ways and Means Committee, which predictably issued a report blasting Biddle's actions and blaming the bank for the suspension of pension payments. In response, the Senate issued a report defending Biddle's decision and criticizing the administration for making the unlawful request. Not only had the Bank War become personal, but it had become so vicious and cynical that even Revolutionary War veterans were fair game.

That April, the Jacksonians in the House, who were that chamber's majority, passed four resolutions attacking the bank. The first prohibited the House from ever rechartering the bank, while two others expressed approval for removing the deposits and placing them in state banks. The final resolution called for the creation of a committee to investigate the bank and determine its role in causing the recession. These resolutions were the product of the Ways and Means Committee, chaired by Tennessee's Polk, a man so close to Jackson politically that he was called "Young Hickory." Jackson was so pleased by the resolutions that he called them "triumphant," crowing that the House action "puts to death, that mamouth [sic] of corruption and power, the Bank of the United States."[80]

Impolitic to the end, Biddle refused to allow the House committee members access to the bank's records. In particular, the investigators wanted to search the bank's correspondence to see if Biddle had bought support for recharter by extending loans to members of Congress. The bank's president decried what he saw as a political ploy instigated by Jackson, complaining, "for the last few years, the executive power of the government has been wielded by a mere gang of banditti. I know these people perfectly, keep the police on them constantly, and in my deliberate judgment there is not on the face of the earth a more profligate crew than those who now govern the president."[81] When Biddle refused to allow the committee members to root through his correspondence or to testify before the committee, the bank's enemies demanded that the House hold Biddle in contempt. Biddle noted the irony of being held in contempt "by the votes of members of Congress because I would not give up to their enemies their confidential letters." Ultimately, cooler heads—in this case Democrats concerned that the Bank War had gone too far—prevailed, and Biddle was not punished for his refusal to cooperate with the House investigation. He even tried to wrest victory from the jaws of defeat by requesting that the Senate conduct its own investigation of the bank. The Senate granted his wish, but by the time the upper chamber's report appeared in December, the midterm elections had passed and, with them, Biddle's chance to win the Bank War.

Yet there was a high cost to Jackson's victory in the Bank War. One of the ironic consequences of Jackson's unremitting war against the bank was that it solidified the various anti-Jacksonian factions into a new political party, the Whigs. Though the Whigs represented a broad coalition—historian Robert Remini described them as "National Republicans, bank men, nullifiers, tariff men, states' righters, former Democrats, and other dissidents"—two things bound them together: opposition to Jackson's bank policy and concern over the president's expansion of executive power.[82] The Whigs took their name from the British Whig Party, which in the late seventeenth century opposed Charles II. In the eighteenth century, the American revolutionaries adopted the name to emphasize their opposition to Great Britain's King George III. Thus, the name Whig denoted opposition to royal authority, a fact that reflected the anti-Jacksonians' main criticism of Jackson—that he acted like a king, making decisions tyrannically. Historians have been unable to determine who first suggested the name, but Jackson's opponents quickly adopted it. Van Buren, worried about the Whigs and about the growing chorus of Democrats who were privately and publicly grumbling about Jackson's war on the bank, counseled the president to back off. Characteristically, Jackson dismissed Van Buren's concerns, condescendingly telling the vice president "your friends may be leaving you—but my friends *never* leave me."[83]

5

A Battle Won,
a War Lost

By summer 1834, it was clear that the Bank War had been decided. Once Congress adjourned in June 1834, Biddle decided to reverse the contractionary policy; his gambit had failed, and there was nothing to be gained in causing additional economic hardship. The bank's change of course did little to ease the hard feelings. In the 1834 midterm elections, the anti-Jacksonian forces picked up twelve seats in the House. Though Jacksonians still controlled that body, it was nonetheless a stinging defeat for the president. However, because the Jacksonians still dominated the House, it was now impossible for Biddle to secure a new charter for the bank before its current one expired on March 4, 1836. Consequently, Biddle explored the possibility of getting a state charter (as opposed to the current federal charter). Such a step had drawbacks: a state charter would only authorize the bank to operate branches within Pennsylvania, and the legislature would almost surely demand a series of expensive concessions.[1] Nevertheless, it was better than closing outright, and Biddle, acting through a series of intermediaries, lobbied quite hard for the state charter.

In early 1836, Biddle applied to the Pennsylvania legislature for a charter to continue operating the Bank of the United States as a state bank. He described the bank as "devotedly attached to [Pennsylvania's] interests and fame" in opposition to New York's pretensions to financial leadership. Jackson's allies in Pennsylvania tried to prevent the legislature from chartering the bank, claiming it would break Old Hickory's heart to see the bank get a second lease on life, but the president was in the last year of his second term, and his influence was diminishing day by day. Pennsylvania's Democrats wanted to heal the bitterness in the party caused by the Bank War and saw chartering the bank as a state institution as one way to do that. Moreover, the legislature demanded a $2 million bonus—essentially a gift of money—from the bank in exchange for the charter. In addition, Biddle was forced to promise to loan the commonwealth up to $6 million to fund canals and railroads and to subscribe to the stock of any private railroad or canal company that the legislature wanted to encourage. Individual legislators also demanded a series of smaller inducements, like promises that Biddle would establish bank branches in their districts. There is even some evidence that Biddle was forced to bribe legislators for their votes. Ironically, the Bank War had turned the Bank of the United States into what Jackson had always claimed it was: a font of bribery and unethical political pressure that served the interests of the political and economic elites at the expense of the common people. Despite these costly promises, Biddle called the charter "very good," describing it as "better in many respects than the present."[2] Diarist Philip Hone rejoiced at the bank's new charter, exclaiming, "[the charter] passed both Houses [of the Pennsylvania legislature], and the Governor . . . having signed it, 'the monster' is on its legs again, and the President must seek his retreat 'in the deserts of Arabia' where he swore he would go whenever the bank was incorporated."[3] That was wishful thinking on Hone's part; the bank's new state charter was hardly the unqualified victory over Jackson that Hone imagined.

Because the bank's new state charter limited its operations to Pennsylvania, Biddle began preparing for the branches' closure. In March 1835, the bank's board of directors ordered some of its branches to stop making loans, and by November, half the branches carried no loans on their books. In August that year, Biddle wrote to a friend that the bank was "winding up its affairs quietly and certainly . . . the great object is to close its concerns in such a manner as to avoid all pressure."4 The easiest way to do this was to sell the various branches to local banks, and Biddle described the process at some length in a letter to a friend:

> We are now making arrangements with several of the new Banks to purchase the whole establishment of the Office near them—banking house, debts & all. This plan is very advantageous to the new Bank which thus succeeds to the standing, capital, deposits & custom of the Office, & the Bank of the U.S. It possesses the attraction of enabling them to close the Office at once. As an example of such a settlement, I will mention what has just taken place at Lexington, Kentucky. The President & Cashier of the Office have been appointed President & Cashier of the Northern Bank of Kentucky—and that Institution has agreed to take the Banking House at the valuation hitherto put upon it in our schedules—& also to take the whole of the current debt.5

The Bank of the United States' stockholders met for the last time February 19, 1836. During the meeting, the directors voted to present Biddle with a gift "in token and commemoration of the gratitude of the stockholders for his faithful, zealous, and fearless devotion to their interests."6

Meanwhile, in autumn 1836, the voters of the United States gratified Jackson's wishes when they elected (barely) his handpicked successor, Vice President Van Buren, president. Though Van Buren's 50.83 percent of the popular vote was hardly a mandate, it still exceeded the total votes of his four Whig challengers, William H. Harrison, Hugh L. White, Daniel Webster, and Willie P. Mangum. The fact that the Whigs ran four candidates in 1836 testifies to the fact that the new party was as riven by internal conflict as the Democrats had been in the 1820s, and its two leaders—Henry Clay and John Calhoun—shared little beyond their antipathy toward Jackson and the fact that they both aspired to the presidency.

Writing to Biddle in early May 1835, Webster predicted that Van Buren would win the presidency the next year because the Whigs were split along sectional lines, with Northern Whigs preferring one candidate and Southern Whigs another, thereby ensuring a Democratic victory.[7] Nevertheless, the Second Party System was born and would dominate American politics for a quarter century. Yet despite his victory in 1836, Van Buren was nowhere near as popular as Jackson, and he went out of his way to identify himself with the outgoing administration, promising to continue Old Hickory's policies if elected.

Jackson was also pleased when, in January 1837, by a vote of 24 to 19, the newly ascendant Democrats erased the Senate's censure of him from its official journal. The censure had been a rallying cry for Democrats ever since it had been passed. Six state legislatures replaced their US senators with men who promised to have the censure reversed,[8] and Jackson's supporters in Congress had repeatedly tried to do so. In January, Democrats again pushed a measure expunging the censure. Not having the numbers to defeat the resolution, the Whigs tried to wear down their opponents by giving speeches until the session adjourned. In his memoirs, Benton notes, "It was evident that consumption of time, delay and adjournment, was their plan." In other words, they were mounting a filibuster, the first in US history. Democratic senators, "fortifying themselves with an ample supply, ready in a nearby committee room, of cold hams, turkeys, beef, pickles, wines, and cups of hot coffee," were determined to wait the Whigs out and advance the resolution to a vote.[9] Seeing they had no chance of success, the Whigs ended their filibuster at about midnight and watched in horror as the Democratic majority voted to expunge the censure of Jackson.[10] Benton moved that the Senate's secretary, Asbury Dickens, carry out the removal immediately. Many Whig senators stomped out of the chamber in disgust, and some observers in the gallery began hissing. Jumping to his feet, Benton yelled, "Bank ruffians! Bank ruffians!" and demanded that the sergeant at arms seize members of the crowd. Once calm was restored, Dickens struck through the censure in the Senate's official journal, writing, "Expunged by order of the Senate, this 16th day of January, 1837."[11]

The Jacksonians' joy at Van Buren's election and the expunging of the Senate censure was short lived. Within weeks of Van Buren's inauguration, the United States plunged into the most severe recession in its history up to that point as a result of a banking panic that originated in New York. The Panic of 1837 was the indirect byproduct of Jackson's economic policies, beginning with his assault on the Bank of the United States. The bank's demise coincided with a rapid expansion in America's economy. For instance, the federal government sold three times the amount of land in 1835 as it had in 1834, encouraged by the dramatic rise in the price of cotton (which increased by 50 percent during the same period).[12] Speculators borrowed money from the state banks, who issued ever larger amounts of bank notes to satisfy the demand for loans. Meanwhile, the states passed ever stricter limits on state banks' note issues. For instance, from 1833 to the end of Jackson's presidency, six states outlawed the emission of notes with a face value below five dollars, while others banned notes below twenty dollars.[13] While notes and coin in small denominations for everyday transactions were scarce, state and federal policies injected a massive amount of liquidity into the system in the form of large denomination notes, ensuring that for land speculators, money was plentiful and therefore cheap; ironically, in the lead-up to the panic, money was both abundant and scarce.

Jackson's antipathy to federally funded internal improvements also contributed to the unchecked expansion of paper money that set in motion the Panic of 1837. In the face of federal unwillingness to invest in American infrastructure, and thereby exercise some oversight on the projects, states undertook them, often in competition with one another. For instance, the success of the Erie Canal in New York threatened Pennsylvania's economic position, so the Keystone State undertook its own canal system. In most cases, states funded these projects by selling bonds, and state bond issues grew rapidly during Jackson's presidency. From 1830 to 1835, state bond issues averaged $8 million, a more than threefold increase of the average annual total during the 1820s. In the last three years of Jackson's presidency, that annual average jumped to $36 million, a 450 percent increase. Put another way, the states were essentially printing money and spending it on massive public works projects. This flood of public spending was not offset by higher taxes, meaning there was more money in circulation, causing inflation and encouraging speculation.[14]

In June 1836, Jackson added fuel to the fire by signing into law the Act to regulate the Deposits of Public Money (generally called the Deposit Act), though according to Benton, he did so "with repugnance of feeling and recoil of judgment," a reflection of the fact that Jackson never went quite far enough to satisfy the locofocos' demands.[15] The Deposit Act mandated that the Treasury Department disburse to state banks $30 million of the approximately $35 million national surplus as loans on the basis of the states' respective representation in Congress. The Deposit Act sharply curtailed the Treasury Department's discretion in selecting pet banks, mandating that at least one bank in each state be designated to receive deposits and setting strict reserve minimums designed to ensure the banks' health. The law also enjoined the secretary of the Treasury from transferring money to the banks for any reason other than disbursements. In other words, the Treasury Department was legally prohibited from using public money to prop up failing banks or to help those banks weather temporary shortages of liquid assets, which tied the department's hands when it came to dealing with the cascade of bank failures caused by the Panic of 1837.[16] Finally, the act required state banks to redeem their notes in specie and prohibited the issuance of notes in denominations below five dollars (this was later raised, first to ten dollars and then in March 1837 to twenty dollars), which only exacerbated the scarcity of low-denomination currency even as high-denomination notes were readily available.[17]

Meanwhile, to fulfill the provisions of the act, Secretary of the Treasury Woodbury scrambled to find additional state banks to receive federal funds, more than doubling the number of deposit institutions, from thirty-six to eighty-one, in the span of six months.

At the same time, he also elected to transfer specie from banks along the Eastern Seaboard to those in the interior, which deprived Eastern merchants of specie at just the moment they needed it to purchase the agricultural products of the South and West. In addition, two weeks after Congress adjourned, the administration promulgated the "order to the Collectors and Disbursers of the Public Money," which has come to be known as the Specie Circular. Under the circular's terms, the federal government would only accept specie for payment of public lands beginning December 15. The Specie Circular's timing was no accident. During the congressional session, Benton had tried to pass a similar bill but was unable to find any support for the measure. So, in a sop to the locofocos, Jackson implemented the policy through executive decree while Congress was in recess.[18]

The Specie Circular was disastrous for a number of reasons. In the first place, it created a federal preference for specie and discriminated against paper money. As we have seen, this had been overissued and had fueled the land speculation that the Specie Circular was designed to check. Jackson's decree rendered these notes essentially worthless, at least as far as purchasing land went. As a result, the value of paper money fell relative to the value of specie, which spurred people to redeem their paper money for specie. This in turn strained the state banks, which (in the absence of any efficient restraint) had overissued bank notes on the theory that they would not have to redeem a substantial portion of the notes at one time. In addition, Jackson claimed to be issuing the circular in response to "frauds, speculations, and monopolies" that threatened "the sound condition of the currency of the country" through "the ruinous extension of bank issues and bank credits," which seemed to imply that at least some of the state banks were insolvent. Since there was no way for the average person to tell which banks had "ruinously" overextended themselves, many citizens responded by hoarding whatever specie still circulated and by redeeming bank notes, which, of course, quickly depressed the notes' value and only reinforced the belief that the banks were in trouble, making it a self-fulfilling prophecy.[19]

Moreover, the circular was the last step in the last battle over the Democratic Party's positions on paper money and banking. Two prominent Democratic senators, New York's Nathaniel P. Tallmadge and Virginia's William C. Rives, were essentially forced out of the party over their opposition to the Specie Circular; both men were eventually reelected to the Senate as Whigs. This incident became a cautionary tale in Democratic circles about the price to be paid for opposing a Democratic president. In 1857, Democratic President James Buchanan tried to intimidate Senator Stephen A. Douglas, a Democrat from Illinois, into quieting his criticism of the administration by saying, "Mr. Douglas, I desire you to remember that no Democrat has ever yet differed from an Administration of his own choice without being crushed. Remember the fate of Tallmadge and Rives."[20]

By the beginning of 1837, all the elements were in place for an economic meltdown of epic proportions. State banks in New York City saw their specie reserves drop by almost 80 percent from September 1, 1836 to May 1 1837, from $7.2 million to $1.5 million.[21] Inflation had increased the price of food to such an extent that workers in New York rioted in February. Worse, concerns over the country's economic health pushed short-term interest rates to nearly 25 percent per year, and by the spring a trickle of business failures became a wave and then a tsunami. As businesses failed, they defaulted on loans, and as the defaults mounted, banks across the country curtailed their lending. Eroding confidence led to a run on New York's banks on May 9, during which more than $600,000 in specie was withdrawn. That evening, rumors circulated that a number of the city's banks were tottering on the brink of insolvency, and the following morning all the city's bank's suspended specie payments. As a result, people began hoarding coins, and specie all but disappeared from circulation, leaving rapidly depreciating bank notes as the only circulating medium. Biddle supported the suspension of specie payments, seeing it as the least-terrible option, and in the days and weeks that followed, he worked to restore confidence in the nation's banks.[22]

In an unexpected turn of events, on May 6, the newly appointed secretary of war, Joel Poinsett, wrote to Biddle and solicited the banker's advice in helping end the depression. Poinsett asked, "Can you not in your financial knowledge and experience devise some plan by which a wholesome control may be exercised over bank issues, and exchanges be brought back to what they were before the destruction of the Bank?"[23] Poinsett's letter to Biddle, which Van Buren almost surely knew about, is further evidence of the essentially political nature of the Bank War, at least for the New Yorker; he opposed the bank when it seemed politically opportune and then turned to Biddle for help once the political winds shifted. For his part, Biddle recommended essentially that the administration "make peace with the Bank," in the hope that doing so would restore faith in the banking sector and the administration, but Van Buren was politically unable to follow this advice.[24]

One interesting element of the Panic of 1837 is that it illustrates how thoroughly New York had supplanted Philadelphia as the nation's banking capital, in large part because of the Bank of the United States' transition to a state-chartered institution. This economic panic, which started in Manhattan, quickly spread across the country. At the time of the panic, the city's deposit banks held more than one-third of the total federal funds disbursed up to that point. This meant that New York's banks had larger specie reserves than all the deposit banks in Alabama, Kentucky, Louisiana, Mississippi, and Tennessee put together.[25] In the five years after the specie suspension (the first nationwide suspension in the country's history), the nation's state banks lost an astonishing 45 percent of the assets on their books, causing more than one in four to close their doors permanently.[26] In short, because of Manhattan's new preeminence in American finance, a panic that started in New York would not long remain there. Within two days of specie suspension in New York, banks in other cities also suspended specie redemption, which sent a shudder through the country's financial system.[27]

On May 12, diarist Philip Hone lamented the worsening economic conditions, noting, "The commercial distress and financial embarrassment pervade the whole nation. Posterity may get out of it, but the sun of the present generation will never again shine out. Things will grow better gradually from the curtailment of business, but the glory has departed." Hone had no doubt who was to blame for these conditions: according to the New Yorker, "Jackson, Van Buren, and Benton form a triumvirate more fatal to the prosperity of America than Caesar, Pompey, and Crassus were to the liberties of Rome."[28]

The banks' suspension of specie redemption effectively killed the pet banking scheme because, under the terms of the Deposit Act, any bank that suspended specie redemption was automatically ineligible to hold federal government funds. As a result, Van Buren was forced to reconvene Congress in September 1837 to devise an alternative system for collecting revenue and paying the nation's bills. In his message to Congress, Van Buren doubled down on Jacksonian economic orthodoxy, asserting, "it is apparent that events of the last few months have greatly augmented the desire, long existing among the people of the United States, to separate the fiscal operations of the government from those of individuals or corporations."[29] Van Buren's message took recharter of the Bank of the United States off the table as an option for dealing with the worsening crisis, and he advocated that the Treasury Department itself take on the task of collecting, housing, and disbursing federal funds.

Hastily, Congress passed a number of bills to deal with the crisis. One authorized the emission of $10 million in Treasury notes (interest-bearing bonds), while another postponed payment of the next portion of the surplus until the department had assembled a list of banks that were actually eligible to receive the funds. In October, Congress passed the Relief Act, which authorized the Treasury Department to continue writing drafts against federal funds held in state banks but also created a process for banks that were unable to redeem those drafts when they were presented. Most important, the Relief Act authorized the Treasury Department to accept, at par value, any notes issued by deposit banks, in the hope that it would restore the notes' value and with it the banks' health. The Relief Act succeeded in helping the deposit banks pay back the government's funds; by the end of the first quarter of 1838, forty-one of the deposit banks had completely repaid the federal deposits. In May 1838,

"Fifty Cents." An anti-Jacksonian cartoon criticizing Jackson and Benton for the shortage of money during the Panic of 1837. Both men ride toward a cliff in pursuit of a butterfly labeled "Gold Humbug," while Van Buren takes another path toward the Bank of the United States. Despite the cartoonist's belief that the panic would force Van Buren to recharter the bank, the new president opted for an independent treasury instead. (*Library of Congress*)

Congress repealed the Specie Circular, and the state banks in turn resumed specie payments. By the end of 1838, more than 90 percent of the federal funds paid out under the Specie Circular had been returned to the Treasury Department, and in early 1841, Secretary Woodbury closed the book on the surplus by writing off the last $500,000 of government money held by deposit banks as uncollectable.[30] Biddle saw the Specie Circular's repeal as vindication of his opposition to the Jackson administration's economic policies, gloating in a letter, "The repeal of the Specie Circular was an actual surrender by the Administration," and he believed that it augured a return of the bank's charter.[31] In this, as in so many other aspects of the Bank War, he had misread the political tea leaves. While Van Buren had been forced to abandon the Specie Circular, there was no way the administration could recharter the Bank of the United States even if it wanted to do so.

Instead, one of the consequences of the pet banking debacle and Congress's subsequent limitation on the Treasury Department's autonomy in choosing banks was to shift Democratic orthodoxy away from using state banks as federal depositories to an independent treasury, or (to its opponents) the subtreasury, scheme. The idea for the independent treasury had been floated by New York Senator Silas Wright as early as 1834, but in the midst of the pet banking scheme it failed to get any traction. In its most basic form, the independent treasury plan imagined the creation of a few dozen Treasury offices in cities around the country where payments could be received and government money disbursed. Democrats argued that it would finally separate the federal government from the banking sector. Biddle ridiculed the idea as "this insane Sub Treasury scheme," claiming that Van Buren intended to "break down all the great interests of the county."[32] The Senate passed the bill handily, and, after multiple false starts, the House followed suit by a small margin on June 30.

The Panic of 1837 and the subsequent depression quickly eroded Van Buren's standing with the voters and support for Jacksonian economic policies. In a measure of how quickly the depression had altered the country's political landscape, Biddle's name was even seriously floated as a potential Whig presidential nominee. In spring 1837, Thomas Cooper, the former president of South Carolina College (later the University of South Carolina), wrote to Biddle, claiming, "The tide is turning strongly against the measures of the last and present Administration. . . . Why not look to the Presidency? Can your name be brought forward at a time more advantageous than at present? You are rising, your opponents are falling: strike the ball on the rebound, and I think this is the moment."[33] Nor was Cooper the only person pushing Biddle to challenge Van Buren. In his response to Cooper, Biddle noted, "I have received from various quarters intimations of a disposition to connect my name with the next election of President." However, Biddle would not run; he told Cooper, "These I have never considered seriously, nor indeed noticed at all: but to you I will speak for the first time without reserve. . . . I am quite sure that I have not the least affectation in saying, that to myself personally, the office has not the slightest attraction. Its dignity has been degraded by the elevation of unworthy men—and as to mere power, I have been for years in the daily exercise of more personal authority than any President habitually enjoys." That being said, Biddle did close the letter by noting that he would do nothing to prevent his friends and supporters from placing his name in contention, only that he would not actively seek the presidency himself.[34] Despite Biddle's tepid refusal to pursue high political office, rumors to the contrary persisted. Following Biddle's resignation from the bank (now called The Bank of the United States of Pennsylvania) in 1839, there were widespread rumors that Van Buren intended to appoint him to the Treasury Department. The fact that such wild fantasies could even be entertained speaks to the depth of the economic troubles facing the nation.[35]

Though the Democrats managed—barely—to maintain control of both houses of Congress in the midterm elections of 1838, they were throttled in 1840. For the first time, the Whigs won control of the Senate and the House, and in both cases by decisive margins. Worse, Van Buren lost his bid for reelection to William Henry Harrison, one of only two Whigs ever elected president. The recession caused by the Panic of 1837—itself a product of banking policies that Van Buren had supported as Jackson's secretary of state and vice president—was largely to blame, with some newspapers going so far as to call him "Martin Van Ruin." Following Harrison's death in April 1841, just one month after his inauguration, his successor, Vice President John Tyler, called Congress into special session to deal with the country's financial system. Tyler had been a Democrat until he ran afoul of the Jackson administration. In his message to Congress, Tyler claimed that Americans had backed Jackson in the latter's war against the Bank of the United States but condemned both the pet banking scheme and the independent treasury plan. Proposing no alternative, Tyler turned the matter over to Congress, saying, "I shall be ready to concur with you in the adoption of such a system as you may propose, reserving to myself the ultimate power of rejecting any measure which may, in my view of it, conflict with the Constitution, or otherwise jeopard[ize] the prosperity of the country."[36] Henry Clay put forward a Senate bill to resurrect the

Bank of the United States, apparently feeling that a Whig president would sign the bill into law. Unfortunately for Clay's bill, Tyler agreed with Jackson's decision to veto the bank's recharter. As a result of this and Clay's unwillingness to compromise on certain aspects of the bill, Tyler twice vetoed it. Enraged, the Whigs expelled the president from the party and even tried to impeach him. Eventually, a House committee led by John Quincy Adams reported that Tyler had committed the "high crime and misdemeanor" of misusing his veto power (one of their favorite complaints about Jackson), but the impeachment resolution failed to pass the House, and Tyler served the rest of his term.

When Democrat James Polk won the presidency in 1844, he had four goals: annex Texas, settle territorial disputes with Great Britain over Oregon, cut the tariff, and reestablish the independent treasury; he succeeded in all four. Under the terms of an act passed by Congress in summer 1846 and signed into law shortly thereafter, all federal funds would be housed either in the Treasury or in one of the various "sub-treasuries" in major cities across the country. Furthermore, the Treasury Department would only accept payment in the form of specie or Treasury notes, which had a tendency to drain specie from the economy and amplify the importance of state bank notes. In other words, he won the battle—he got the independent treasury system—but lost the war, at least in the sense that the federal government was now even more closely tied to the banking system than during Biddle's day.

With only minor modifications during the Civil War and the Gilded Age, the independent treasury system remained the country's approach to collecting its revenue and paying its bills until the early twentieth century. Historians have not been kind to the eighty years between the end of the Bank War and the inauguration of the Federal Reserve System: Richard Timberlake Jr. noted that the period between the bank's transition to a state bank and the creation of the Federal Reserve System in 1913 is generally regarded by scholars "as the Dark Ages of monetary policy," while Edwin J. Perkins placed the blame for the turbulent nature of American banking in the last two-thirds of the nineteenth century on the Bank War, noting that the confrontation between Jackson and Biddle so politicized the development of the nation's financial institutions "that it defied political solution until the creation of the Federal Reserve in the twentieth century." David Kinley, who wrote the most thorough study of the independent treasury system that more or less dominated American finance in one form or another until well into the twentieth century, called the system "injurious to the business interests of the country."[37]

After a heady twenty-year-and-two-month association with the Bank of the United States, Biddle resigned the presidency on March 29, 1839, asserting "the right to claim the relaxation and repose which approaching age and precarious health require." The bank's financial position, which had been precarious due to the Panic of 1837 and the depression that followed, had improved substantially in the months leading up to Biddle's resignation. Shortly after leaving, he noted to a friend, "the affairs of the institution [are] in a state of great prosperity and in the hands of able directors and officers."[38] And the stockholders were so pleased with his policies that they presented him a beautiful set of china as a retirement gift. Philip Hone described the stockholders' gift to Biddle: "I was shown this afternoon, at the shop of Messrs. Fletcher & Co., in Chestnut street, the most superb service of plate I ever saw, to be presented by the directors of the old Bank of the United States to Mr. Nicholas Biddle. It is to cost $15,000. The inscription recites all of his valuable services to the institution and to the country at large, and among other things his having 'created the best currency *in the world.*'"[39]

Fatigue was not the only reason Biddle left the bank in 1839. According to his biographer, Biddle was seriously considering challenging Van Buren for president in the election of 1840. Believing that more than a decade of Jacksonian economic policies had weakened the country, and seeing no one among the Whigs who had either the skill or the popular support to do anything about it, Biddle cautiously but deliberately encouraged his friends and allies to promote his candidacy. Unfortunately for Biddle, the bank's economic health proved illusory: In spring 1839, the country fell back into recession, largely due to economic developments in Europe; this recession was far more severe than the one immediately following the Panic of 1837 and destroyed any hope that Biddle (whose appeal was built on his close association with the banking system) would win the presidency in 1840. In fact, public anger quickly focused on Biddle, with one Philadelphia diarist noting, "Have been amused to hear people talk about Biddle, once the idol, the god of Philadelphia, upon whom for years every specimen of flattery and attention was accorded, and whom not to speak of as the greatest man of these times was regarded as flat blasphemy."[40]

Biddle's successor as the bank's president, Thomas Dunlap, actively worked to convince the institution's stockholders that the challenges it faced were his predecessor's fault. Focusing on a series of loans the Bank of the United States made while Biddle was its president, a small group of stockholders argued that he had misused the institution's funds for his own gain. There was little evidence to support these charges, but on February 4, 1841, Pennsylvania delivered the bank a deathblow by first borrowing $800,000 from the institution, which the bank paid in notes, and then immediately redeeming those notes for specie. The move drained the bank's specie reserves, forcing it to suspend note redemption, and it closed its doors. This, coupled with the lingering controversy about Biddle's lending policies, led many observers to believe that the banker had been involved in something unsavory during his term as the institution's president, implicitly reinforcing all of the negative charges made by the Jacksonians. As a result, Biddle was even tried for fraud. He was acquitted, but that did nothing to salvage his reputation, and he died soon afterward, at age fifty-eight, on February 27, 1844. At the time of his death, Biddle's reputation was permanently destroyed. One diarist claimed Biddle "can persuade, delight, humbug, and beguile, but he cannot convince, elevate, inspire or command.... [I]f Mr. Biddle had possessed or displayed the really great qualities, men would not have withdrawn from him their respect and confidence and admiration when the game turned against him and his prosperity was gone."[41]

Conclusion

The Bank of the United States' final liquidation in 1841 is as good a place as any to end a narrative history of the Bank War, but that event was in no way the end of the story: the reverberations from Biddle and Jackson's showdown echoed throughout the remainder of the nineteenth century. That the Bank War was a critical moment in US political history second only to the Civil War can hardly be argued, for, as the preceding pages have chronicled, the conflict gave birth to the Second Party System by crystallizing the Democratic Party and thus causing the formation of the opposition Whig Party. The conflict, which quickly became the leading issue of the 1832 presidential election, involved all the leading political figures of the day, and Jackson's victory that year in no way ended the debate. If this was the Bank War's only claim to fame, it would certainly deserve a new narrative history such as the one you are holding.

However, as I asserted in the introduction, I believe the Bank War's importance goes beyond merely the immediate political ramifications I described above. The Bank War exposed some of the most important and enduring tensions in American history. The first of these is the inherent tension between democratic accountability and technocratic competence. On the one hand, the Founding Fathers created a federal government that was designed to insulate policymakers from the ever-shifting winds of public opinion and thereby create a space where legislators and presidents could act in the country's best interests (even if doing so meant bucking public opinion). The rise of American democracy in the first decades of the nineteenth century was a rebuke to this elitist vision of republican governance. Democrats like Jackson argued that governing required no special skills, and therefore, any white man of average intelligence could successfully perform the duties of a public servant. Implicitly, the Democrats argued that government officials should act in ways consistent with public opinion, though as the Bank War makes clear, these same officials were frequently willing to use the press in order to mold (some might say manipulate) public opinion to support their preferred policies. This tension endures to the current day and is reflected in the political controversy over the Federal Reserve's role in the American economy.

On a more fundamental level, the Bank War was one in a long series of conflicts over the "proper" interpretation of the powers of the federal government that goes back to the country's very founding and is embodied in the struggle between the Hamiltonians' broad interpretation and the Jeffersonians' strict constructionism of the Constitution. Does the Constitution implicitly grant to Congress the right to do all things "necessary and proper" to exercise the powers ascribed to it by that document, or is the federal government limited to only the powers expressly defined in that document? As I noted in chapters 3 and 4, we can see elements of this debate in Jackson's critique of the Bank of the United States' charter, and the Bank War in no way settled this debate. It rages to the current day, in large part because there is no "objectively" correct answer to the question.

Finally, I think the Bank War offers us two important lessons about American history that we, as citizens, forget at our peril. The first is that politics and political debates were not somehow "better," "cleaner," or more dignified in the past. If anything, the politics of the Jacksonian era, which the Bank War did so much to shape, were more aggressive and pugnacious than contemporary American political discourse. While it is comforting to believe as so many Americans do that the past was a "paradise lost" of civil political nonpartisan statesmanship, the reality is far different.

The second lesson about American history builds on the first, and it is the price to be paid when partisanship and ideology override pragmatism and flexibility. As the debate over the Bank of the United States devolved into a winner-take-all fight to the political death, the combatants lost any sense of perspective. Jackson, Clay, Calhoun, Van Buren, and eventually even the scrupulously nonpartisan Biddle were willing to play political games with the economy in order to "beat" the other "team." The ultimate loser was the United States, which was plagued throughout the nineteenth century by ineffective financial sectors that encouraged a boom-and-bust economy that persisted well into the twentieth century. In a hyperpartisan and ideological age, it is worth recalling that failure to compromise and a focus on "beating" one's political opponents rather than governing responsibly has a cost that often exceeds the current election cycle.

Epilogue

The Bank War was one of the defining events in American political and economic life in the nineteenth century. Second only in importance to the Civil War, it was a battle waged by some of the most colorful characters in American history. Their stories do not end with the shuttering of the Bank of the United States in 1841.

ANDREW JACKSON

After he left office in March 1845, Jackson returned to the Hermitage, where he lived for the rest of life. Though he was widely blamed for the Panic of 1837 and the resulting depression, the return of good economic times in the 1840s improved his public image. He remained engaged in politics until his death, corresponding with up-and-coming Democrats, including future President James K. Polk. In retirement, Jackson lost none of the pugnacity and emotion that had characterized his political career. He died June 8, 1845, at age seventy-eight, managing to outlive the much younger Biddle by more than a year.

MARTIN VAN BUREN

In 1844, the Democrats rejected Van Buren and instead nominated James K. Polk (known as "Little Hickory" for his close relationship with Andrew Jackson). Polk narrowly beat his Whig opponent, Henry Clay, and as president undertook an ambitious agenda that included passage of a version of Van Buren's independent treasury plan. Meanwhile, Van Buren gravitated toward abolitionism throughout the mid-1840s as another of Polk's signature policies, the annexation of Texas, aggravated sectional tension over slavery. In 1848, the antislavery faction of the Democratic Party (known as the "barnburners") and the Free Soil Party (so named because it opposed slavery) nominated Van Buren for president. Van Buren won no electoral votes, but he bested the regular Democratic nominee, Lewis Cass, in New York, thereby allowing Whig candidate Zachary Taylor to become president. During the 1850s, Van Buren returned to the Democratic fold, although he never abandoned his abolitionist principles, and during the Civil War he publicly supported President Abraham Lincoln's unionist policies. Van Buren died in July 1862, at his New York estate, at age seventy-nine.

ROGER B. TANEY

After the Senate rejected Taney's nomination to be secretary of the Treasury in June 1834, Jackson looked for ways to reward the Marylander's faithful service. In January 1835, Associate Justice of the Supreme Court Gabriel Duvall retired from the bench, creating a vacancy that Jackson nominated Taney to fill. Taney's nomination arrived in a Senate unchanged from the previous summer and, if anything, less willing to work with Jackson than before. Senate Whigs successfully blocked a vote on Taney's nomination before the session ended in March and even went so far as to propose the abolition of Duvall's seat. This proposal went nowhere, however, and former House Speaker Philip Pendleton Barbour's nomination to fill Duvall's seat was confirmed in early 1836. Chief Justice John Marshall died July 6, 1835, and Jackson nominated Taney that December, this time to be chief justice. Senators Clay, Webster, and Calhoun led a spirited opposition to Taney's nomination, but they could not overcome the fact that the Democrats were now in the majority. On March 15, 1836, the Senate confirmed Taney's nomination and granted him his commission. Taney's twenty-eight-year tenure on the court was one of the most eventful in American legal history. Joining the other justice appointed by Jackson, Taney moved the court away from the expansive nationalism and government activism of the Marshall court and earned lasting ignominy for himself by writing the majority decision in the infamous Dred Scott case.

In *Dred Scott v. Sanford*, the Supreme Court was asked to determine whether a slave taken by his or her master into free territory and then later returned to slavery was still a slave. The implications of this question were huge: if slaves became free simply by journeying to a free state, it could create a tidal wave of slave escapes. The court's decision, which Taney wrote, reaffirmed the lower court's ruling that transporting a slave into a free state did not emancipate the slave, who remained the property of his or her owner. In addition, the court, for only the second time in its history, found an act of Congress unconstitutional. In this case, it was the portions of the 1820 Missouri Compromise that had attempted to set hard and fast rules about whether territories becoming states could enter the Union as free or slave states. The practical effect of this action was moot because Congress had replaced the Missouri Compromise with the Compromise of 1850, but it is certainly worth noting that Taney exercised a court prerogative that he had criticized as part of the Jackson administration in the 1830s.

The Dred Scott decision contributed to the sectional tension over slavery and led abolitionist John Brown to try to foment a slave uprising by seizing the federal arsenal at Harpers Ferry in 1859. After the Civil War broke out in 1861, Taney proved to be a thorn in Lincoln's side. When the administration suspended the writ of habeas corpus in Maryland, Taney ruled that only Congress had that authority. Taking a page from Jackson's playbook, Lincoln ignored Taney's ruling. The chief justice spent his last few years mired in poverty (despite his $10,000 annual salary) and ill health. He died at age eighty-seven on October 13, 1864. Lincoln made no statement on Taney's passing and did not attend the chief justice's funeral, a personal slight reminiscent of Jackson.

HENRY CLAY

The poor economy and Van Buren's general unpopularity convinced Clay to make another bid for the presidency in 1840, but he lost the Whig nomination to William Henry Harrison, who won the general election but died a month after his inauguration. Four years later, Clay managed to get the nomination, but he lost in the general election to James K. Polk largely due to his opposition to the annexation of Texas. Clay feared (rightly, as it turned out) that annexation of Texas would enflame the debate over slavery and potentially lead to a civil war. The Kentuckian hoped to succeed Polk in 1848 but lost the Whig nomination to Zachary Taylor, a general and hero of the Mexican-American War. However, Clay remained an important figure in national politics and played a leading role in negotiating the Compromise of 1850, which seemed, at the time of his death, to have finally settled the controversy over the expansion of slavery. He died in Washington on June 29, 1852, at age seventy-five.

JOHN C. CALHOUN

After he resigned the vice presidency on December 26, 1832, Calhoun was reelected to the Senate, where he proved to be a thorn in Jackson's side for the rest of Old Hickory's term. Taking an increasingly hard line on states' rights and slavery, Calhoun emerged as the peculiar institution's most important defender in Congress, at one point calling it a "positive good." He supported Van Buren's independent treasury scheme but remained personally antagonistic to the New Yorker. In 1844, President Tyler named Calhoun secretary of state. In that role, Calhoun was a polarizing presence, turning the debate over the annexation of Texas into a fight over slavery. Returning to the Senate after Tyler's term ended, Calhoun opposed the Compromise of 1850, seeing it as an attack on Southern states' rights. He died in Washington on March 31, 1850, at age sixty-six.

DANIEL WEBSTER

Following his victory in the presidential election of 1844, Harrison named Webster his secretary of state, a position he continued to hold under Tyler. Webster remained in the cabinet even after all his

Whig colleagues resigned in 1841 over Tyler's veto of the national bank bill, but he resigned under pressure in May 1843. Two years later, he returned to the Senate and supported the Compromise of 1850. That same year, President Millard Fillmore appointed Webster secretary of state, a position he held until 1852. Webster desperately wanted to be the Whig presidential nominee in 1852, but his support of the Compromise of 1850 alienated many abolitionists who succeeded in denying him the nomination. Their opposition did not matter in the end: Webster died at age seventy on October 24, 1852, after falling from his horse.

Notes

INTRODUCTION

1. David Kinley, *The History, Organization, and Influence of the Independent Treasury of the United States* (New York: Greenwood, 1968), 1.
2. Martin Van Buren, *The Autobiography of Martin Van Buren*, ed. John Clement Fitzpatrick (Washington, DC: Government Printing Office, 1920), 2:626.
3. Walter Buckingham Smith, *Economic Aspects of the Second Bank of the United States* (Cambridge, MA: Harvard University Press, 1953), 150.
4. Robert V. Remini, *Andrew Jackson and the Bank War: A Study in the Growth of Presidential Power* (New York: Norton, 1967), 154–5.
5. Arthur M. Schlesinger Jr., *The Age of Jackson* (Boston: Little, Brown, 1945), 92.
6. Smith, *Economic Aspects*, 150.

CHAPTER 1: A BANK FOR THE UNITED STATES

1. H. W. Brands, *The Money Men: Capitalism, Democracy, and the Hundred Years' War over the American Dollar* (New York: Norton, 2006), 23.
2. Edward S. Kaplan, *The Bank of the United States and the American Economy* (Westport, CT: Greenwood, 1999), 3.
3. Ibid., 28.
4. Remini, *Jackson and the Bank War*, 35.
5. Dallas to Calhoun, December 24, 1815, *Niles Register* 9, quoted in Thomas Payne Govan, *Nicholas Biddle: Nationalist and Public Banker, 1786–1844* (Chicago: University of Chicago Press, 1959), 50.
6. Remini, *Jackson and the Bank War*, 35; Govan, *Nicholas Biddle*, 28.
7. Kaplan, *Bank of the United States*, 21.
8. Broadus Mitchell, *Alexander Hamilton: A Concise Biography* (New York: Oxford University Press, 1976), 90–1.
9. John F. Chown, *A History of Money: From AD 800* (New York: Routledge, 1994), 161.
10. Brands, *Money Men*, 51.
11. Richard H. Timberlake Jr., "The Specie Standard and Central Banking in the United States before 1860," *Journal of Economic History* 21, no. 3 (September 1961): 321.
12. Quoted in Dumas Malone, *Jefferson and the Ordeal of Liberty* (Boston: Little, Brown, 1962), 364.

13. Kaplan, *Bank of the United States*, 29.

14. Ibid., 39.

15. Ibid., 42.

16. Ibid., 45.

17. Ibid. 38.

18. Kinley, *History, Organization*, 16.

19. William J. Schultz and M. R. Caine, *Financial Development of the United States* (New York: Prentice-Hall, 1937), 182.

20. Raymond Walters Jr., "The Origins of the Second Bank of the United States," *Journal of Political Economy*, vol. 53 no. 2 (June 1945): 115–6.

21. Ibid., 126.

22. Kaplan, *Bank of the United States*, 54–5.

23. Walters, "Origins of the Second Bank," 130.

24. Daniel Webster, *Speeches and Forensic Arguments*, 8th ed., vol. 1 (Boston: Tappan, Whitemore, and Mason, 1848), 223.

25. Walters, "Origins of the Second Bank," 123; Govan, *Nicholas Biddle*, 51.

26. Govan, *Nicholas Biddle*, 51.

27. Leon M. Schur, "The Second Bank of the United States and the Inflation after the War of 1812," *Journal of Political Economy* 68, no. 2 (April 1960): 118.

28. Kaplan, *Bank of the United States*, 58.

29. Schur, "Second Bank," 120.

30. Smith, *Economic Aspects*, 101.

31. Kaplan, *Bank of the United States*, 70.

CHAPTER 2: THE ERA OF GOOD FEELINGS

1. Philip Hone, *The Diary of Philip Hone* (New York: Library Editions, 1970), 239.

2. Alexis de Tocqueville, *Democracy in America*, 8th ed. (New York: Pratt, Woodford, 1848), 316.

3. Quoted in Govan, *Nicholas Biddle*, 115.

4. Kaplan, *Bank of the United States*, 102.

5. Remini, *Jackson and the Bank War*, 43.

6. Jefferson to William Short, January 8, 1825, in *The Works of Thomas Jefferson: Correspondence and Papers, Volume 12: 1816-1826*, ed. Paul Leicester Ford (New York: G. P. Putnam's Sons, 1905), 392.

7. Donald B. Cole, *The Presidency of Andrew Jackson* (Lawrence: University Press of Kansas, 1993), 15.

8. Biddle to Smith, December 29, 1828, Biddle Papers, Library of Congress, quoted in Govan, *Nicholas Biddle*, 107.

9. Quoted in Mark R. Cheathem, *Andrew Jackson and the Rise of Democrats* (Santa Barbara, CA: ABC-Clio, 2015), 186.

10. Quoted in Cheathem, *Andrew Jackson*, 186.

11. A. J. Langguth, *Driven West: Andrew Jackson and the Trail of Tears to the Civil War* (New York: Simon & Schuster, 2010), 96.

12. Cole, *Presidency of Andrew Jackson*, 19.

13. Govan, *Nicholas Biddle*, 111.

14. Quoted in ibid., 4.

15. Ibid., 79. Others have described Biddle in less complimentary, though certainly accurate, ways. According to historian George Shortt, Biddle was "too self-confident and often too arrogant to have possessed either the tact or conciliatory temper necessary" to avoid conflict with Jackson. George E. Shortt, "The Second Bank of the United States under Two Charters" (PhD diss., University of Chicago, 1929), 50.

16. Govan, *Nicholas Biddle*, 11–12; Kinley, *History, Organization*, 10.

17. Govan, *Nicholas Biddle*, 57.

18. Ibid.

19. Kaplan, *Bank of the United States*, 59.

20. Schur, "Second Bank,"122; Timberlake, "Specie Standard," 328.

21. Biddle to Monroe, January 24, 1819, Monroe Papers, Library of Congress, quoted in Govan, *Nicholas Biddle*, 58.

22. Govan, *Nicholas Biddle*, 59.

23. Shortt, "Second Bank, 53.

24. David M. Wright, "Langdon Cheves and Nicholas Biddle: New Data for a New Interpretation," *Journal of Economic History* 13, no. 3 (Summer 1953): 306–7.

25. Govan, *Nicholas Biddle*, 60.

26. Biddle to Crawford, December 8, 1819, Biddle Papers, Library of Congress, quoted in Govan, *Nicholas Biddle*, 61; Wright, "Langdon Cheves," 308.

27. Govan, *Nicholas Biddle*, 67.

28. Frank Otto Gatell, "Secretary Taney and the Baltimore Pets: A Study in Banking and Politics," *Business History Review* 39, no. 2 (Summer 1965): 206.

29. Govan, *Nicholas Biddle*, 75.

30. Ibid., 78.

31. Quoted in Shortt, "Second Bank," 54.

32. Kaplan, *Bank of the United States*, 92.

33. Ibid., 83.

34. Reginald Charles McGrane, *The Panic of 1837: Some Financial Problems of the Jacksonian Era* (New York: Russell & Russell), 95.

35. Kaplan, *Bank of the United*, 86.

36. Kinley, *History, Organization*, 10.

37. Remini, *Jackson and the Bank War*, 35; Kaplan, *Bank of the United States*, x.

38. Smith, *Economic Aspects*, 135.

39. Quoted in Kaplan, *Bank of the United States*, 85

40. Ibid., 83.

41. Colt to Biddle, January 28, 1823, Biddle Papers, Library of Congress, quoted in Govan, *Nicholas Biddle*, 89.

42. Richard H. Timberlake Jr., "The Specie Circular and Distribution of the Surplus," *Journal of Political Economy* 68, no. 2 (April 1960): 112.

43. Thomas P. Govan, "Fundamental Issues of the Bank War," *Pennsylvania Magazine of History & Biography* 82, no. 3 (July 1958): 308.

44. Smith, *Economic Aspects*, 125.

45. Stockholder to Biddle, June 17, 1828, in Nicholas Biddle, *The Correspondence of Nicholas Biddle Dealing with National Affairs, 1807–1844*, ed. Reginald Charles McGrane (Boston: Houghton Mifflin, 1919), 51.

46. Quoted in Govan, *Nicholas Biddle*, 144; Harry N. Scheiber, comp., "Some Documents on Jackson's Bank War," *Pennsylvania History: A Journal of Mid-Atlantic Studies* 30, no. 1 (January 1963): 46.

47. Govan, *Nicholas Biddle*, 144.

48. Quoted in ibid., 137.

49. Kaplan, *Bank of the United States*, 109.

50. John M. McFaul, *The Politics of Jacksonian Finance* (Ithaca, NY: Cornell University Press, 1972), 26.

51. Quoted in Cole, *Presidency of Andrew Jackson*, 195.

52. Biddle to White, November 27, 1827, in Biddle, *Correspondence*, 42–3.

53. Quoted in Shortt, "Second Bank," 80.

54. Ibid.

55. Quoted in Robert V. Remini, *Andrew Jackson: The Course of American Democracy, 1833–1845* (New York: Harper & Row, 1984), 98.

56. Arthur Fraas, "The Second Bank of the United States: An Instrument for an Interregional Monetary Union." *Journal of Economic History* 34, no. 2 (June 1974): 447.

57. Smith, *Economic Aspects*, 61.

Chapter 3: Scandals, Vetoes, and a Looming Crisis

1. Cole, *Presidency of Andrew Jackson*, 6.

2. Biddle to Hoffman, December 22, 1828, in Biddle, *Correspondence*, 62.

3. Colt to Biddle, January 7, 1829, in Biddle, *Correspondence*, 66.

4. Cole, *Presidency of Andrew Jackson*, 57–8.

5. Jackson to Overton, June, 8, 1829, in Jacob Dickinson Papers, Tennessee State Library, quoted in Remini, *Jackson and the Bank War*, 45.

6. Biddle to Samuel Smith, December 29, 1828, Buddle, *Correspondence*, 63.

7. Smith, *Economic Aspects*, 153.

8. Govan, *Nicholas Biddle*, 209.

9. Brands, *Money Men*, 61.

10. Chown, *History of Money*, 168.

11. McFaul, *Politics of Jacksonian Finance*, 56.

12. Hone, *Diary*, 351

13. Van Buren to Thomas Ritchie, January 13, 1827, Martin Van Buren Papers, Library of Congress.

14. Quoted in Cole, *Presidency of Andrew Jackson*, 52.

15. Biddle to Cooper, May 6, 1833, in Biddle, *Correspondence*, 209.

16. Quoted in Govan, *Nicholas Biddle*, 116.

17. McLean to Biddle, January 5, 1829, in Biddle, *Correspondence*, 64.

18. Biddle to McLean, January 11, 1829, Biddle Papers, Library of Congress, quoted in Remini, *Jackson and the Bank War*, 51.

19. Biddle to McLean, January 10, 1829, in Biddle, *Correspondence*, 76.

20. Nathan Sargent, *Public Men and Events from the Commencement of Mr. Monroe's Administration, in 1817, to the Close of Mr. Fillmore's, in 1853* (Philadelphia: J. B. Lippincott, 1875), 1:217.

21. Biddle to Dickens, September 16, 1829, in Biddle, *Correspondence*, 76.

22. Quoted in James Parton, *Life of Andrew Jackson* (New York: Mason Brothers, 1860), 3:264.

23. Cheathem, *Andrew Jackson*, 188–9.

24. Biddle to Dickens, September 16, 1829, Biddle Papers, Library of Congress, quoted in Remini, *Jackson and the Bank War*, 54.

25. Bruce Ambacher, "George M. Dallas and the Bank War." *Pennsylvania History: A Journal of Mid-Atlantic Studies* 42 no. 2 (April 1, 1975), 123.

26. Smith, *Economic Aspects*, 65.

27. Andrew Jackson, "Veto Message, May 27, 1830, American Presidency Project, accessed June 5, 2015, http://www.presidency.ucsb.edu/ws/?pid=67036.

28. "Memorandum," in Biddle, *Correspondence*, 93.

29. Biddle to Gales, March 2, 1831, in Biddle, *Correspondence*, 125.

30. Carl B. Swisher, "Roger B. Taney's 'Bank War Manuscript,'" *Maryland Historical Magazine* 53, no. 2 (June 1958): 109.

31. Quoted in Govan, *Nicholas Biddle*, 123.

32. Cole, *Presidency of Andrew Jackson*, 59.

33. Kaplan, *Bank of the United States*, 107–8.

34. Quoted in Govan, *Nicholas Biddle*, 126.

35. Quoted in Kaplan, *Bank of the United States*, 112.

36. Quoted in Cheathem, *Andrew Jackson*, 189.

37. Quoted in Smith, *Economic Aspects*, 5.

38. Quoted in Govan, *Nicholas Biddle*, 120.

39. Parton, *Life of Andrew Jackson*, 1:vii.

40. Quoted in Cheathem, *Andrew Jackson*, 267–8.

41. Quoted in Kaplan, *Bank of the United States*, 109.

42. Ibid.

43. Quoted in Govan, *Nicholas Biddle*, 125.

44. Quoted in Kaplan, *Bank of the United States*, 110.

45. Cole, *Presidency of Andrew Jackson*, 97.

46. Quoted in Govan, *Nicholas Biddle*, 126.

47. Quoted in Kaplan, *Bank of the United States*, 110.

48. Ibid., 111.

49. Biddle to Smith, January 2, 1830, in Biddle, *Correspondence*, 94; Biddle to Dickens, September 16, 1829, in Biddle, *Correspondence*, 75–6.

50. Lewis to Biddle, October 16, 1829, in Biddle, *Correspondence*, 80.

51. Cheathem, *Andrew Jackson*, 191.

52. Biddle to Silabee, December 7, 1829, in Biddle, *Correspondence*, 92.

53. Jon Meacham, *American Lion: Andrew Jackson in the White House* (New York: Random House, 2008), 115.

54. Cole, *Presidency of Andrew Jackson*, 37.

55. Ibid., x.

56. Ibid., 39.

57. Jackson, "Veto Message: May 27, 1830."
58. Ibid.
59. Lewis to Biddle, May 25, 1830, in Biddle, *Correspondence*, 104.
60. Quoted in Kaplan, *Bank of the United States*, 112.
61. Ibid.
62. Clay to Biddle, June 14, 1830, in Biddle, *Correspondence*, 105.
63. Andrew Jackson, "Second Annual Message," December 6, 1830, *American Presidency Project*, accessed June 6, 2015, http://www.presidency.ucsb.edu/ws/?pid=29472.
64. Quoted in Kaplan, *Bank of the United States*, 113.
65. Quoted in Govan, *Nicholas Biddle*, 129.
66. Cheathem, *Andrew Jackson*, 192; Swisher, "Taney's 'Bank War Manuscript,'" 2:115.
67. Cole, *Presidency of Andrew Jackson*, 87, 93.
68. Ibid., 88.
69. Quoted in Govan, *Nicholas Biddle*, 162, 163.
70. Andrew Jackson, "Third Annual Message," December 6, 1831, *American Presidency Project*, accessed June 6, 2015, http://www.presidency.ucsb.edu/ws/?pid=29473.
71. Van Buren, "Autobiography," 600–1.
72. Swisher, "Taney's 'Bank War Manuscript," 2: 215.
73. Ibid., 109.
74. Quoted in Govan, *Nicholas Biddle*, 170.
75. Quoted in Remini, *Jackson and the Bank War*, 75.
76. Amos P. Kendall, *Autobiography of Amos P. Kendall*, ed. William Stickney (Boston: Lee and Shepard, 1872), 516.
77. Quoted in Kaplan, *Bank of the United States*, 114.
78. Ibid., 114.
79. Ibid., 115.
80. Quoted in Ambacher, "George M. Dallas," 126.
81. James L. Crouthamel, "Three Philadelphians in the Bank War: A Neglected Chapter in American Lobbying" *Pennsylvania History: A Journal of Mid-Atlantic Studies* 27, no. 4 (October, 1960): 365.
82. Govan, *Nicholas Biddle*, 135.
83. Quoted in Kaplan, *Bank of the United States*, 116.
84. Cole, *Presidency of Andrew Jackson*, 100.
85. Quoted in Remini, *Jackson and the Bank War*, 75.
86. Ibid., 77.
87. Quoted in Kaplan, *Bank of the United States*, 122.

CHAPTER 4: THE PRESIDENT VERSUS THE BANKER

1. Van Buren, *Autobiography*, 2:625.
2. Frank Otto Gatell, "Sober Second Thoughts on Van Buren, the Albany Regency, and the Wall Street Conspiracy," *Journal of American History* 53, no. 1 (June 1966), 29.
3. Quoted in Remini, *Jackson and the Bank War*, 117.

4. Govan, *Nicholas Biddle*, 137.

5. Quoted in ibid., 138.

6. Thomas Hart Benton, *Thirty Years View: Or a History of the Working of the American Government for Thirty Years from 1820 to 1850* (New York: D. Appleton, 1854), 1:266.

7. Quoted in Kaplan, *Bank of the United States*, 122.

8. Kaplan, *Bank of the United States*, 122–3.

9. Ibid., 124.

10. Quoted in ibid.

11. Quoted in Cheathem, *Andrew Jackson*, 202.

12. Quotes in the following discussion of the veto message are from Andrew Jackson, "President Jackson's Veto Message Regarding the Bank of the United States; July 10, 1832," Avalon Project, accessed June 7, 2015, http://avalon. law.yale.edu/19th_century/ajveto01.asp.

13. Cole, *Presidency of Andrew Jackson*, 113.

14. Quoted in Cheathem, *Andrew Jackson*, 202.

15. Quoted in Cheathem, *Andrew Jackson*, 208.

16. Ibid., 202.

17. Quoted in Kaplan, *Bank of the United States*, 125.

18. Quoted in Govan, *Nicholas Biddle*, 261.

19. Biddle to Clay, August 1, 1832, in Biddle, *Correspondence*, 196.

20. Quoted in Kaplan, *Bank of the United States*, 126.

21. Quoted in ibid., 126–7.

22. McFaul, *Politics of Jacksonian Finance*, 2–3.

23. Ibid., 36.

24. Kaplan, *Bank of the United States*, 128.

25. Andrew Jackson, "Fourth Annual Message," December 4, 1832, *American Presidency Project*, accessed June 8, 2015, http://www.presidency.ucsb.edu/ws/?pid=29474.

26. Cole, *Presidency of Andrew Jackson*, 187.

27. Quoted in Kaplan, *Bank of the United States*, 129

28. Swisher, "Taney's 'Bank War Manuscript,'" 2:108.

29. Carl B., Swisher, ed. "Roger B. Taney's 'Bank War Manuscript.'" *Maryland Historical Magazine* 53, no. 3 (September 1958): 222.

30. Philip Shriver Klein, *President James Buchanan: A Biography* (University Park: Pennsylvania State University Press, 1962), 103.

31. Jackson, "Fourth Annual Message."

32. "President Jackson's Proclamation Regarding Nullification, December 10, 1832," Avalon Project, accessed June 8, 2015, http://avalon.law.yale.edu/19th_century/jack01.asp.

33. Quoted in Cheathem, *Andrew Jackson*, 206.

34. Quoted in Govan, *Nicholas Biddle*, 226.

35. Swisher, "Taney's 'Bank War Manuscript,'" 2:121.

36. Quoted in Remini, *Jackson and the Bank War*, 119.

37. Quoted in Govan, *Nicholas Biddle*, 241.

38. Kaplan, *Bank of the United States*, 130.

39. Ibid., 131.

40. Cole, *Presidency of Andrew Jackson*, 85.

41. Quoted in Kaplan, *Bank of the United States*, 131.

42. Alfred Steinberg, *The First Ten: The Founding Presidents and Their Administrations* (Garden City, NY: Doubleday, 1967), 328.

43. Frank O. Gatell, "Secretary Taney and the Baltimore Pets: A Study in Banking and Politics," *Business History Review* 39, no. 2 (Summer 1965), 207.

44. Robert Rutland, *The Democrats: From Jefferson to Clinton* (Columbia: University of Missouri Press, 1995), 63.

45. Andrew Jackson, "Fifth Annual Message," December 3, 1833, *American Presidency Project*, accessed June 9, 2015, http://www.presidency.ucsb.edu/ws/?pid=29475.

46. Hone, *Diary*, 83.

47. Quoted in Kaplan, *Bank of the United States*, 133.

48. Hone, *Diary*, 82.

49. Quoted in Remini, *Jackson and the Bank War*, 125.

50. Swisher, "Taney's 'Bank War Manuscript," 3:218.

51. Govan, *Nicholas Biddle*, 215

52. Frank O. Gatell, "Spoils of the Bank War: Political Bias in the Selection of Pet Banks," *American Historical Review* 70, no. 1 (October 1964): 38; Harry N. Scheiber, "The Pet Banks in Jacksonian Politics and Finance, 1833–1841," *Journal of Economic History* 23, no. 2 (June 1963): 199.

53. Stuart Bruchey, ed., "Roger Brooke Taney's Account of His Relations with Thomas Ellicott in the Bank War," *Maryland Historical Magazine* 53 (March 1958), 62.

54. Gatell, "Spoils of the Bank War," 41, 43.

55. Quoted in Govan, *Nicholas Biddle*, 250.

56. Scheiber, "Pet Banks," 200.

57. McFaul, *Politics of Jacksonian Finance*, 78.

58. Quoted in ibid., 75.

59. Ibid., 63.

60. Scheiber, "Pet Banks," 199.

61. Howard Bodenhorn, "Small-Denomination Banknotes in Antebellum America," *Journal of Money, Credit and Banking* 25, no. 4 (November 1993): 814.

62. Kinley, *History, Organization*, 16.

63. Quoted in Cole, *Presidency of Andrew Jackson*, 96.

64. Quoted Kaplan, *Bank of the United States*, 133.

65. Ibid.

66. Jacob P. Meerman, "The Climax of the Bank War: Biddle's Contraction, 1833–34," *Journal of Political Economy* 71, no. 4 (August 1963): 378.

67. Cheathem, *Andrew Jackson*, 209.

68. David A. Martin, "Metallism, Small Notes, and Jackson's War with the B.U.S.," *Explorations in Economic History* 11, no. 3 (1974): 232–3.

69. Kaplan, *Bank of the United States*, 134.

70. Parton, *Life of Andrew Jackson*, 3:549–550.

71. Hone, *Diary*, 87.
72. Andrew Jackson, "Message to the Senate Protesting Censure Resolution," April 15, 1834, American Presidency Project, accessed June 9, 2015, http://www.presidency.ucsb.edu/ws/index.php?pid=67039#axzz1h5Kt09IY.
73. Andrew Jackson, "President Jackson's Message of Protest to the Senate; April 15, 1834," Avalon Project, accessed June 14, 2015,
http://avalon.law.yale.edu/19th_century/ajack006.asp.
74. Hone, *Diary*, 96.
75. Cole, *Presidency of Andrew Jackson*, 208.
76. Quoted in Kaplan, *Bank of the United States*, 144.
77. Quoted in ibid., 147.
78. Quoted in McGrane, *Panic of 1837*, 5.
79. Remini, *Jackson and the Bank War*, 160.
80. Quoted in Kaplan, *Bank of the United*, 143.
81. Quoted in Govan, *Nicholas Biddle*, 291.
82. Remini, *Jackson and the Bank War*, 129.
83. Quoted in ibid., 153.

CHAPTER 5: A BATTLE WON, A WAR LOST

1. Colt to Biddle, November 13, 1834, in Biddle, *Correspondence*, 245-6.
2. Govan, *Nicholas Biddle*, 285.
3. Hone, *Diary*, 199.
4. Kaplan, *Bank of the United States*, 148.
5. Biddle to Huske, August 6, 1835, in Biddle, *Correspondence*, 254.
6. Kaplan, *Bank of the United States*, 148.
7. Webster to Biddle, May 9, 1835, in Biddle, *Correspondence*, 250.
8. Senators were not elected by the people until the twentieth century.
9. William M. Meigs, *The Life of Thomas Hart Benton* (Philadelphia: J. B. Lippincott, 1904), 237-8.
10. Martin B. Gold and Dimple Gupta, "The Constitutional Option to Change Senate Rules and Procedures: A Majoritarian Means to Overcome the Filibuster," *Harvard Journal of Law & Public Policy* 28, no. 1 (Winter 2005): 216.
11. Remini, *Andrew Jackson: The Course of America Democracy*, 174.
12. McGrane, *Panic of 1837*, 5.
13. Bodenhorn, "Small-Denomination Banknotes," 815.
14. Cole, *Presidency of Andrew Jackson*, 67.
15. Quoted in Remini, *Andrew Jackson: The Course of America Democracy*, 169.
16. Scheiber, "Pet Banks," 203.
17. Remini, *Andrew Jackson: The Course of America Democracy*, 170; Gatell, "Spoils of the Bank War," 36.
18. Timberlake, "Specie Circular," 110.
19. Scheiber, "Pet Banks," 206, 207.
20. Robert Walter Johannsen, *Stephen A. Douglas* (Urbana: University of Illinois Press, 1997), 586.
21. Peter L. Rousseau, "Jacksonian Monetary Policy, Specie Flows, and the Panic of 1837," *Journal of Economic History* 62, no. 2 (June 2002): 458.

22. Govan, *Nicholas Biddle*, 313; Bruchey, "Roger Brooke Taney's Account," 59.

23. Quoted in Govan, *Nicholas Biddle*, 310.

24. Biddle to Poinsett, May 8, 1837, in Biddle, *Correspondence*, 274.

25. Rousseau, "Jacksonian Monetary Policy," 463.

26. Ibid., 457.

27. McGrane, *Panic of 1837*, 97.

28. Hone, *Diary*, 258.

29. Kinley, *History, Organization*, 22–3.

30. Scheiber, "Pet Banks," 211.

31. Biddle to Jaudon, June 23, 1838, in Biddle, *Correspondence*, 314.

32. Biddle to Clay, February 3, 1838, in Biddle, *Correspondence*, 299.

33. Cooper to Biddle, April 29, 1837, in Biddle, *Correspondence*, 272.

34. Biddle to Cooper, May 8, 1837, in Biddle, *Correspondence*, 278.

35. Hone, *Diary*, 351.

36. Kinley, *History, Organization*, 30.

37. Timberlake, "Specie Standard," 318; Edwin J. Perkins, "Lost Opportunities for Compromise in the Bank War: A Reassessment of Jackson's Veto Message," *Business History Review* 61, no. 4 (Winter 1987): 531; Kinley, *History, Organization*, iii.

38. Govan, *Nicholas Biddle*, 350, 351.

39. Hone, *Diary*, 288.

40. Govan, *Nicholas Biddle*, 367.

41. Ibid., 384.

Bibliography

PRIMARY SOURCES

Benton, Thomas Hart. *Thirty Years' View: Or a History of the Working of the American Government for Thirty Years from 1820 to 1850.* Vol. 1. New York: D. Appleton, 1854.

Biddle, Nicholas. *The Correspondence of Nicholas Biddle Dealing with National Affairs, 1807–1844.* Edited by Reginald Charles McGrane. Boston: Houghton Mifflin, 1919.

Bruchey, Stuart, ed. "Roger Brooke Taney's Account of His Relations with Thomas Ellicott in the Bank War." *Maryland Historical Magazine* 53, March 1958.

Calhoun, John C. *The Papers of John C. Calhoun: 1829–1832.* Edited by Clyde N. Wilson. Vol. 11. Columbia: University of South Carolina Press, 1978.

Calhoun, John C., and Clyde N. Wilson. *The Papers of John C. Calhoun: 1833–1835.* Vol. 12. Columbia: University of South Carolina Press, 1979.

Clay, Henry, Robert Seager, and Melba Porter Hay. *The Papers of Henry Clay: Candidate, Compromiser, Whig, March 5, 1829–December 31, 1836.* Vol. 8. Lexington: University Press of Kentucky, 1984.

Clay, Henry, Robert Seager, Melba Porter Hay, and Mary W. M. Hargreaves. *The Papers of Henry Clay. January 1, 1828–March 4, 1829.* Lexington: University Press of Kentucky, 1982.

De Tocqueville, Alexis. *Democracy in America.* 8th ed. New York: Pratt, Woodford, 1848.

Hone, Philip. *The Diary of Philip Hone.* New York: Library Editions, 1970.

Jackson, Andrew. "Fifth Annual Message." December 3, 1833. American Presidency Project. http://www.presidency.ucsb.edu/ws/?pid=29475

———. "Fourth Annual Message." December 4, 1832. American Presidency Project. http://www.presidency.ucsb.edu/ws/?pid=29474.

————. "Message to the Senate Protesting Censure Resolution." April 15, 1834. American Presidency Project. http://www.presidency.ucsb.edu/ws/index.php?pid=67039#axzz1h5Kt 09IY.

————. *The Papers of Andrew Jackson: 1829*. Edited by Daniel Feller. Vol. 7. Knoxville: University of Tennessee Press, 2007.

————. *The Papers of Andrew Jackson: 1830*. Edited by Daniel Feller, Laura-Eve Moss, and Thomas Coens. Vol. 8. Knoxville: University of Tennessee Press, 2010.

————. *The Papers of Andrew Jackson: 1831*. Edited by Daniel Feller, Thomas Coens, Laura-Eve Moss, and Erik Alexander. Vol. 9. Knoxville: University of Tennessee Press, 2013.

————. "President Jackson's Message of Protest to the Senate; April 15, 1834." Avalon Project. http://avalon.law.yale.edu/19th_century/ajack006.asp.

————. "President Jackson's Proclamation Regarding Nullification, December 10, 1832." Avalon Project. http://avalon.law.yale.edu/19th_century/jack01.asp.

————. "President Jackson's Veto Message Regarding the Bank of the United States; July 10, 1832." Avalon Project. http://avalon.law.yale.edu/19th_century/ajveto01.asp.

————. "Second Annual Message," December 6, 1830. American Presidency Project. http://www.presidency.ucsb.edu/ws/?pid=29472.

————. "Third Annual Message," December 6, 1831. American Presidency Project. http://www.presidency.ucsb.edu/ws/?pid=29473.

————. "Veto Message," May 27, 1830. American Presidency Project. http://www.presidency.ucsb.edu/ws/?pid=67036.

Jefferson, Thomas. *The Works of Thomas Jefferson: Correspondence and Papers, Volume 12: 1816–1826*. Edited by Paul Leicester Ford. New York: G. P. Putnam's Sons, 1905.

Kendall, Amos P. *Autobiography of Amos P. Kendall*. Edited by William Stickney. Boston: Lee and Shepard, 1872.

Sargent, Nathan. *Public Men and Events from the Commencement of Mr. Monroe's Administration, in 1817, to the Close of Mr. Fillmore's, in 1853*. Vol. 1. Philadelphia: J. B. Lippincott, 1875.

Schieber, Harry N., comp. "Some Documents on Jackson's Bank War." *Pennsylvania History: A Journal of Mid-Atlantic Studies* 30, no. 1 (January 1963).

Van Buren, Martin. *The Autobiography of Martin Van Buren*. Vol. 2. Edited by John Clement Fitzpatrick. Washington: Government Printing Office, 1920.

————. Martin Van Buren Papers, Library of Congress.

Webster, Daniel. *The Papers of Daniel Webster: Correspondence, 1830–1834.* Edited by Charles M. Wiltse. Vol. 3. Hanover, NH: Published for Dartmouth College by the University Press of New England, 1977.

———. *Speeches and Forensic Arguments.* 8th ed. Vol. 1. Boston: Tappan, Whitemore, and Mason, 1848.

SECONDARY SOURCES

Ambacher, Bruce. "George M. Dallas and the Bank War." *Pennsylvania History: A Journal of Mid-Atlantic Studies* 42, no. 2 (April 1, 1975): 116–35.

Bartlett, Marguerite Gold. *The Chief Phases of Pennsylvania Politics in the Jacksonian Period.* Allentown, PA: H. R. Haas, 1919.

Belohlavek, John M. "Dallas, the Democracy, and the Bank War of 1832." *Pennsylvania Magazine of History & Biography* 96, no. 3 (July 1972): 377–90.

———. *George Mifflin Dallas: Jacksonian Patrician.* University Park: Pennsylvania State University Press, 1977.

Bodenhorn, Howard. *A History of Banking in Antebellum America: Financial Markets and Economic Development in an Era of Nation-building.* Cambridge: Cambridge University Press, 2000.

———. "Small-Denomination Banknotes in Antebellum America." *Journal of Money, Credit and Banking* 25, no. 4 (November 1993): 812–27.

———. *State Banking in Early America: A New Economic History.* New York: Oxford University Press, 2003.

Bowers, Douglas E. "From Logrolling to Corruption: The Development of Lobbying in Pennsylvania, 1815–1861." *Journal of the Early Republic* 3, no. 4 (December 1, 1983): 439–74.

Brands, H. W. *The Money Men: Capitalism, Democracy, and the Hundred Years' War over the American Dollar.* New York: Norton, 2006.

Bruchey, Stuart Weems. *Enterprise: The Dynamic Economy of a Free People.* Cambridge, MA, and London: Harvard University Press, 1990.

Cheathem, Mark R. *Andrew Jackson and the Rise of the Democrats.* Santa Barbara, CA: ABC-Clio, 2015.

Chown, John F. *A History of Money: From AD 800.* New York: Routledge, 1994.

Cole, Donald B. *The Presidency of Andrew Jackson.* Lawrence: University Press of Kansas, 1993.

Crouthamel, James L. "Three Philadelphians in the Bank War: A Neglected Chapter in American Lobbying." *Pennsylvania History: A Journal of Mid-Atlantic Studies* 27, no. 4 (October 1, 1960): 361–78.

Daniels, Belden L. *Pennsylvania, Birthplace of Banking in America.* Harrisburg, PA: Pennsylvania Bankers Association, 1976.

Earle, Jonathan H. *Jacksonian Antislavery and the Politics of Free Soil: 1824–1854.* Chapel Hill, NC, and London: University of North Carolina Press, 2004.

"Economic Change and Political Realignment in Antebellum Pennsylvania." *Pennsylvania Magazine of History and Biography* 113, no. 3 (July 1, 1989): 347–95.

Engerman, Stanley L. "A Note on the Economic Consequences of the Second Bank of the United States." *Journal of Political Economy* 78, no. 4 (July/August 1970): 725–28.

Ershkowitz, Herbert, and William G. Shade. "Consensus or Conflict? Political Behavior in the State Legislatures during the Jacksonian Era." *Journal of American History* 58, no. 3 (December 1971): 591–621.

Fogel, Robert William, and Stanley L. Engerman. *The Reinterpretation of American Economic History.* New York: Harper & Row, 1971.

Fraas, Arthur. "The Second Bank of the United States: An Instrument for an Interregional Monetary Union." *Journal of Economic History* 34, no. 2 (June 1974): 447–67.

Gatell, Frank Otto. "Money and Party in Jacksonian America: A Quantitative Look at New York City's Men of Quality." *Political Science Quarterly* 82, no. 2 (June 1967): 235–52.

———. "Secretary Taney and the Baltimore Pets: A Study in Banking and Politics." *Business History Review* 39, no. 2 (Summer 1965): 205–27.

———. "Sober Second Thoughts on Van Buren, the Albany Regency, and the Wall Street Conspiracy." *Journal of American History* 53, no. 1 (June 1966): 19–40.

———. "Spoils of the Bank War: Political Bias in the Selection of Pet Banks." *American Historical Review* 70, no. 1 (October 1964): 35–58.

Geisst, Charles R. *Wall Street: A History.* New York: Oxford University Press, 1997.

Gold, Martin B., and Dimple Gupta. "The Constitutional Option to Change Senate Rules and Procedures: A Majoritarian Means to Overcome the Filibuster." *Harvard Journal of Law & Public Policy* 28, no. 1 (Winter 2005): 206–272.

Gordon, John Steele. *Hamilton's Blessing: The Extraordinary Life and Times of Our National Debt.* New York: Walker, 1997.

Govan, Thomas P. "Fundamental Issues of the Bank War." *Pennsylvania Magazine of History & Biography* 82, no. 3 (July 1958): 305–15.

———. *Nicholas Biddle: Nationalist and Public Banker, 1786–1844.* Chicago: University of Chicago Press, 1959.

Hailperin, Herman. "Pro-Jackson Sentiment in Pennsylvania, 1820–1828." *Pennsylvania Magazine of History and Biography* 50, no. 3 (1926): 193–240.

Hammond, Bray. *Banks and Politics in America, from the Revolution to the Civil War*. Princeton: Princeton University Press, 1957.

———. "Jackson, Biddle, and the Bank of the United States." *Journal of Economic History* 7, no. 1 (May 1947): 1–23.

———. "Jackson's Fight with the 'Money Power.'" *American Heritage* 7 (June 1956): 8–11.

Heidler, David Stephen, and Jeanne T. Heidler. *Henry Clay: The Essential American*. New York: Random House, 2010.

Hepburn, A. Barton, and Emily Eaton Hepburn. *A History of Currency in the United States*. New York: A. M. Kelley, 1967.

Hidy, R. W. "The House of Baring and the Second Bank of the United States, 1826–1836." *Pennsylvania Magazine of History & Biography* 68, no. 3 (July 1944): 269–85.

Howe, Daniel Walker. *What Hath God Wrought: The Transformation of America, 1815–1848*. New York: Oxford University Press, 2007.

Inskeep, Steve. *Jacksonland: President Andrew Jackson, Cherokee Chief John Ross, and a Great American Land Grab*. New York: Penguin, 2015.

Jackson, Andrew, John Spencer Bassett, and David Maydole Matteson. *Correspondence of Andrew Jackson*. Washington, DC: Carnegie Institution of Washington, 1926.

Johannsen, Robert Walter. *Stephen A. Douglas*. Urbana: University of Illinois Press, 1997.

Kaplan, Edward S. *The Bank of the United States and the American Economy*. Westport, CT: Greenwood, 1999.

Killenbeck, Mark Robert. *M'Culloch v. Maryland: Securing a Nation*. Lawrence: University Press of Kansas, 2006.

Kindleberger, Charles Poor, and Robert Z. Aliber. *Manias, Panics and Crashes: A History of Financial Crises*. Basingstoke, UK: Palgrave Macmillan, 2005.

Kinley, David. *The History, Organization, and Influence of the Independent Treasury of the United States*. New York: Greenwood, 1968.

Klein, Philip Shriver. *President James Buchanan: A Biography*. University Park: Pennsylvania State University Press, 1962.

Lane, Carl. *A Nation Wholly Free: The Elimination of the National Debt in the Age of Jackson*. Yardley: Westholme, 2014.

Langguth, A. J. *Driven West: Andrew Jackson and the Trail of Tears to the Civil War*. New York: Simon & Schuster, 2010.

Lind, Michael. *Land of Promise: An Economic History of the United States.* New York: Broadside Books, 2012.

Madeleine, M. Grace. *Monetary and Banking Theories of Jacksonian Democracy.* Port Washington, NY: Kennikat, 1970.

Malone, Dumas. *Jefferson and the Ordeal of Liberty.* Boston: Little, Brown, 1962.

Martin, David A. "Metallism, Small Notes, and Jackson's War with the B.U.S." *Explorations in Economic History* 11, no. 3 (1974): 227–47.

McCormick, Richard Patrick. *The Second American Party System: Party Formation in the Jacksonian Era.* Chapel Hill: University of North Carolina Press, 1966.

McFaul, John M. "The Outcast Insider: Reuben M. Whitney and the Bank War." *Pennsylvania Magazine of History & Biography* 91, no. 2 (April 1967): 115–44.

———. *The Politics of Jacksonian Finance.* Ithaca, NY: Cornell University Press, 1972.

McGrane, Reginald Charles. *The Panic of 1837: Some Financial Problems of the Jacksonian Era.* New York: Russell & Russell, 1965.

Meacham, Jon. *American Lion: Andrew Jackson in the White House.* New York: Random House, 2008.

Meerman, Jacob P. "The Climax of the Bank War: Biddle's Contraction, 1833–34." *Journal of Political Economy* 71, no. 4 (August 1963): 378–88.

Meigs, William M. *The Life of Thomas Hart Benton.* Philadelphia: J. B. Lippincott, 1904.

Meyers, Marvin. *The Jacksonian Persuasion: Politics and Belief.* Stanford, CA: Stanford University Press, 1957.

Mihm, Stephen. "The Fog of War: Jackson, Biddle and the Destruction of the Bank of the United States." In *A Companion to the Era of Andrew Jackson.* Edited by Sean Patrick Adams. Malden, MA: Wiley-Blackwell, 2013, 348–75.

———. *A Nation of Counterfeiters: Capitalists, Con Men, and the Making of the United States.* Cambridge, MA: Harvard University Press, 2007.

Miller, Harry E. *Banking Theories in the United States before 1860.* Cambridge, MA: Harvard University Press, 1927.

Mitchell, Broadus. *Alexander Hamilton: A Concise Biography.* New York: Oxford University Press, 1976.

Moulton, R. K. *Legislative and Documentary History of the Banks of the United States from the Time of Establishing the Bank of North America, 1781, to October 1834, with Notes and Comments.* New York: G. & C. Carvill, 1834.

Mueller, Henry Richard. *The Whig Party in Pennsylvania*. Vol. 101. New York: Columbia University, 1922.

Parton, James. *Life of Andrew Jackson*. Vols. 1 and 3. New York: Mason Brothers, 1860.

———. *The Presidency of Andrew Jackson*. Edited with an introduction and notes by Robert V. Remini. New York: Harper & Row, 1967.

Perkins, Edwin J. "Lost Opportunities for Compromise in the Bank War: A Reassessment of Jackson's Veto Message." *Business History Review* 61, no. 4 (Winter 1987): 531–50.

Peterson, Merrill D. *The Great Triumvirate: Webster, Clay, and Calhoun*. New York: Oxford University Press, 1987.

Phillips, Kim T. "The Pennsylvania Origins of the Jackson Movement." *Political Science Quarterly* 91, no. 3 (1976): 489–508.

Plous, Howard J. "Jackson, the Bank War, and Liberalism." *Southwestern Social Science Quarterly* 38, no. 2 (September 1957): 99–110.

Remini, Robert V. *Andrew Jackson and the Bank War: A Study in the Growth of Presidential Power*. New York: Norton, 1967.

———. *Andrew Jackson: The Course of American Democracy, 1833–1845*. New York: Harper & Row, 1984.

Richards, Leonard L. *The Slave Power: The Free North and Southern Domination, 1780–1860*. Baton Rouge: Louisiana State University Press, 2000.

Roberts, Alasdair. *America's First Great Depression: Economic Crisis and Political Disorder after the Panic of 1837*. Ithaca, NY: Cornell University Press, 2012.

Roberts, Jonathan. "Notes and Documents: Memoirs of a Senator from Pennsylvania: Jonathan Roberts, 1771–1854." *Pennsylvania Magazine of History and Biography* 61, no. 4 (October 1937): 446–74; 62, no. 1 (January 1, 1938): 64–97; 62, no. 2 (April 1938): 213–48; 62, no. 3 (July 1938): 361–409; 62, no. 4 (October 1938): 502–51.

Rothbard, Murray N. *A History of Money and Banking in the United States: The Colonial Era to World War II*. Auburn, AL: Ludwig Von Mises Institute, 2005.

Rousseau, Peter L. "Jacksonian Monetary Policy, Specie Flows, and the Panic of 1837." *Journal of Economic History* 62, no. 2 (2002): 457–88.

Rutland, Robert. *The Democrats: From Jefferson to Clinton*. Columbia: University of Missouri Press, 1995.

Ryon, Roderick N. "Moral Reform and Democratic Politics: The Dilemma of Roberts Vaux." *Quaker History* 59, no. 1 (Spring 1970): 3–14.

Scheiber, Harry N. "The Pet Banks in Jacksonian Politics and Finance, 1833–1841." *Journal of Economic History* 23, no. 2 (June 1963): 196–214.

Schlesinger, Arthur M. *The Age of Jackson*. Boston: Little, Brown, 1945.

Schultz, William J., and M. R. Caine. *Financial Development of the United States*. New York: Prentice-Hall, 1937.

Schur, Leon M. "The Second Bank of the United States and the Inflation after the War of 1812." *Journal of Political Economy* 68, no. 2 (April 1960): 118–34.

Sellers, Charles G. "Banking and Politics in Jackson's Tennessee, 1817–1827." *Mississippi Valley Historical Review* 41, no. 1 (1954): 61–84.

Shade, William G. "Politics and Parties in Jacksonian America." *Pennsylvania Magazine of History & Biography* 110, no. 4 (October 1966): 483–507.

Sharp, James Roger. *The Jacksonians versus the Banks: Politics in the States after the Panic of 1837*. New York: Columbia University Press, 1970.

Shelling, Richard I. "Philadelphia and the Agitation in 1825 for the Pennsylvania Canal." *Pennsylvania Magazine of History and Biography* 62, no. 2 (1938): 175–204.

Shenton, James P. *Robert John Walker: A Politician from Jackson to Lincoln*. New York: Columbia University Press, 1961.

Shortt, George E. "The Second Bank of the United States under Two Charters." PhD diss., University of Chicago, 1929.

Sklansky, Jeffrey. "The Moneylender as Magistrate: Nicholas Biddle and the Ideological Origins of Central Banking in the United States." *Theoretical Inquiries in Law* 11, no. 1 (2010): 319–359.

Smith, Culver H. *The Press, Politics, and Patronage: The American Government's Use of Newspapers, 1789–1875*. Athens: University of Georgia Press, 1977.

Smith, Elbert B. *Francis Preston Blair*. New York: Free Press, 1980.

Smith, Walter Buckingham. *Economic Aspects of the Second Bank of the United States*. Cambridge, MA: Harvard University Press, 1953.

Snyder, Charles McCool. *The Jacksonian Heritage: Pennsylvania Politics, 1833–1848*. Harrisburg: Pennsylvania Historical and Museum Commission, 1958.

Steele, Henry. "The Life and Public Service of Governor George Wolfe, 1777–1840." *Proceedings and Addresses of the Pennsylvania German Society* 39 (1930): 5–25.

Steinberg, Alfred. *The First Ten: The Founding Presidents and Their Administrations*. Garden City, NY: Doubleday, 1967.

Stenberg, Richard R. "Jackson, Buchanan, and the 'Corrupt Bargain' Calumny." *Pennsylvania Magazine of History and Biography* 58, no. 1 (1934): 61–85.

Swisher, Carl B., ed. "Roger B. Taney's 'Bank War Manuscript.'" *Maryland Historical Magazine* 53, no. 2 (June 1958): 103–30; 53, no. 3 (September 1958): 215–37.

Sylla, Richard E. "American Banking and Growth in the Nineteenth Century: A Partial View of the Terrain." *Explorations in Economic History* 9 (Winter 1971–2): 202–06.

Temin, Peter. "The Economic Consequences of the Bank War." *Journal of Political Economy* 76, no. 2 (March/April 1968): 257–74.

Timberlake, Richard H., Jr. "The Specie Circular and Distribution of the Surplus." *Journal of Political Economy* 68, no. 2 (April 1960): 109–17.

———. "The Specie Standard and Central Banking in the United States before 1860." *Journal of Economic History* 21, no. 3 (September 1961): 318–41.

Vitiello, Domenic, and George E. Thomas. *The Philadelphia Stock Exchange and the City It Made*. Philadelphia: University of Pennsylvania Press, 2010.

Walters, Raymond, Jr.. "The Origins of the Second Bank of the United States." *Journal of Political Economy* 53, no. 2 (June 1945): 115–31.

Walton, Joseph S. "Nominating Conventions in Pennsylvania." *American Historical Review* 2, no. 2 (1897): 262–78.

Ward, John William. *Andrew Jackson, Symbol for an Age*. New York: Oxford University Press, 1955.

Widmer, Edward L. *Martin Van Buren*. New York: Times Books, 2005.

Wilburn, Jean Alexander. *Biddle's Bank: the Crucial Years*. New York: Columbia University Press, 1967.

Wilentz, Sean. *The Rise of American Democracy: Jefferson to Lincoln*. New York: Norton, 2005.

Wilson, Major L. "The 'Country' versus the 'Court': A Republican Consensus and Party Debate in the Bank War." *Journal of the Early Republic* 15, no. 4 (Winter 1995): 619–47.

———. *The Presidency of Martin Van Buren*. Lawrence: University Press of Kansas, 1984.

Woodford, Frank B. *Lewis Cass: The Last Jeffersonian*. New Brunswick, NJ: Rutgers University Press, 1950.

Wright, David M. "Langdon Cheves and Nicholas Biddle: New Data for a New Interpretation." *Journal of Economic History* 13, no. 3 (Summer 1953): 305–19.

Wright, Robert E. *The First Wall Street: Chestnut Street, Philadelphia, and the Birth of American Finance*. Chicago: University of Chicago Press, 2005.

Zachary, Alan M. "Social Disorder and the Philadelphia Elite before Jackson." *Pennsylvania Magazine of History & Biography* 99, no. 3 (January 1975): 288–308.

Acknowledgments

Projects like *The Bank War* reflect the assistance of dozens, if not hundreds, of people whose names do not appear on the book's cover. In particular, I want to thank Shawn Allan, Chris "Burno" Burns, Jared Cram, Hudson Davis, Saurabh Desai, Joe "Gus Dickson" Haughton, Tanying Dong, Julian Elias, Alissa Fisher, Kelley and Patrick Flynn, Karinne Grabowski, Jennifer Havey, Michael Heinsdorf, Jamie Herbert, John Holz, Victoria King, Stephanie Matulich, Omar Perze, reness Posey, and Wilhemina Letty Watson, all of whom provided friendship and emotional support while I was writing this book. In addition, I would like to thank Tara Snyder Murphy, who read the galleys and made sure I crossed every "t" and dotted every "i;" undoubtedly, *The Bank War* is a much better book because of her help. Next, I want to thank my wife Jennifer and our children Alec and Zoe, all of whom "picked up the slack" around the house so that I could have the time to write. Finally, I want to thank my brother, Andrew, who has consistently supported my scholarly work and has been a reliable and indefatigable booster for years. *The Bank War* is dedicated to him.

Index